Gender questions

Gender questions

Biblical manhood and womanhood
in the contemporary world

John Benton

EVANGELICAL PRESS

EVANGELICAL PRESS
Faverdale North Industrial Estate, Darlington, DL3 0PH, England

Evangelical Press USA
P. O. Box 84, Auburn, MA 01501, USA

e-mail: sales@evangelical-press.org

web: www.evangelical-press.org

First published 2000

British Library Cataloguing in Publication Data available

ISBN 0 85234 462 7

Printed and bound in Great Britain by Creative Print & Design, Ebbw Vale

Contents

		Page
Introduction		7
1.	Freedom and dignity for us all (Gen. 1:26-28)	11
2.	Man according to the Bible (Gen. 2:4-25)	28
3.	Woman according to the Bible (Gen. 2:4-25)	45
4.	Head of the family? (Eph. 5:21-33)	64
5.	The church as family (1 Tim. 3:1-16)	83
Appendix I — The deacons: a brief summary of the biblical teaching		99
Appendix II — Women deacons: an explanation of the New Testament passages		103
Appendix III — Work, family and church?		106

Introduction

The feminist tide was a movement born out of genuine frustrations on the part of women.

> When ... we ask why the existence of one-half of the species should be merely ancillary to that of the other — why each woman should be a mere appendage to a man, allowed to have no interests of her own that there may be nothing to compete in her mind with his interests and his pleasure; the only reason that can be given is that men like it. It is agreeable to them that men should live for their own sake, women for the sake of men.

So wrote Harriet Taylor Mill, the friend and later wife of the philosopher John Stuart Mill. He also took up the cause of women's rights in his pamphlet *The Subjection of Women* (1869).

In some ways women's lot has improved in society since the nineteenth century. However, in other ways it has not. Women's-rights activists would point to recent cases in which women have eventually ended up murdering their husbands, feeling that this was the only way to free themselves from the abuse and physical attacks suffered at the hands of their partners. These are truly wicked situations and indicate that feminist ideas often arise from legitimate grievances and that frequently men and their ways have been the trouble.

So the solution, say many people, is to legislate away all distinctions as far as possible between male and female. This tide of opinion is running very strongly. It is a very fast-flowing tide which is changing the landscape of society in deep and drastic ways. Furthermore, it all seems so right to so many people that even to question it as the proper solution to the problem is precarious, to say the least. It is to invite moral indignation and hostility.

It cannot be denied that many women are treated unfairly. There are acute problems which should command sympathy. But is the 'equality' legislation package the answer? Is the blurring of gender really progress? Will it actually bring about a better deal in society for women? Or is this all a fallacy?

This little book arose out of a teaching series at Chertsey Street Baptist Church in Guildford, as I endeavoured, as a pastor there, to address questions and pressures that were worrying some of the younger people among us. A couple of the chapters included here have appeared in slightly extended form as my contribution to the symposium *Men, Women and Authority* (Day One Publications). I also must acknowledge a huge debt to the book *Recovering Biblical Manhood and Womanhood* (Crossway Publications, 1991), edited by Wayne Grudem and John Piper. It is a book that every Christian ought to study. However, that is a very large volume with which few Christians with busy lives will feel able to grapple. So, although I cover much of the same ground, I feel that this present slim volume might have its uses.

John Benton,
Guildford

Questions

1. As far as you are concerned, what are the greatest injustices surrounding gender issues in society and the church which need to be righted?

2. Meditate on the general principle behind Jesus' words in Mark 3:25. In the light of tensions between men and women, what implications does this verse have for families, churches and society?

I.

Freedom and dignity for us all

Genesis 1:26-28

If you are a Bible-believing Christian you may feel yourself very torn over the issue of the roles of men and women in modern society. You sympathize deeply with women who are frustrated or unfairly treated. On the other hand, you may well feel very uneasy about the tide of opinion which treats men and women as if there were little or no difference between them. Androgyny does not seem to sit very well alongside many strands of thought and statements in the Bible.

We have to ask, 'What does God's Word have to say on this matter of male and female?' This is what this book focuses on. You may be a traditionalist, or you may be a progressive in this whole matter, but wherever you stand personally, God's Word is bound to challenge you. We are all on a pilgrimage of understanding. We believe that in Jesus Christ there is a better way for men and women than ever the secular world could manufacture. The Bible is the Word of God to us, and God loves us and knows us through and through. We can therefore proceed with hope and expectancy. The heavenly Father does not give evil gifts to his children.

This topic is a minefield for many reasons. It is a subject that evokes deep emotions. For the woman who has been physically abused there is understandable anger. For the woman who feels blocked in her career aspirations because of what she sees as male domination of business or commerce, there is an inner turmoil. But over against this, for the man who wishes to support his family, who has been beaten to a job simply, he reckons, because the company has a policy of preferential promotion of women, there is also bitterness. Perhaps in this instance, the successful woman candidate has a husband who already earns a large salary. 'They have two salaries while I have none, and I have children to support!' thinks the embittered man. Such situations are highly charged! It is for these very reasons that we need to hear the Word of God on this subject.

Presuppositions

Before we get into the details of what Scripture says on male and female and their relationship, we need first to look at some fundamental perspectives and assumptions which underlie our arguments. Genesis 1:26-28 provides the starting-point for any Christian consideration of this subject.

> Then God said, 'Let us make man in our image, in our likeness, and let them rule over the fish of the sea and the birds of the air, over the livestock, over all the earth, and over all the creatures that move along the ground.'

> So God created man
>   in his own image,
> in the image of God
>   he created him;
>   male and female
>   he created them.

> God blessed them and said to them, 'Be fruitful and increase in number; fill the earth and subdue it. Rule over

the fish of the sea and the birds of the air and over every living creature that moves on the ground.'

The human race is God's creation: 'Let us *make* man in our image.' These verses form a kind of sandwich in which verse 27 is the filling. The opening verse gives us God's decision to make mankind and the purpose for which we were made — namely, under the authority of God, to rule over the world. Verse 27 states the fact and nature of our creation by God. Then in verse 28 God blesses mankind and the purpose for which we were made is restated.

The *creation* of human beings is our starting-point. When people come to consider any problem, they bring with them various assumptions or presuppositions. Our presuppositions are of immense importance and very often can make the difference between finding a solution to the problem and being unable to solve it. For example, do you know the answer to this little conundrum?

```
.   .   .

.   .   .

.   .   .
```

How can you cover all nine dots with four straight lines without taking your pen from the paper or retracing lines?

The answer is like this:

Now if in thinking about it you inadvertently made the assumption that you could not move your pen-lines outside the square of the dots the problem would be insoluble. But if you made the presupposition that you can move outside the square then the answer is not too difficult to see. The presuppositions we make in approaching any problem are, therefore, very important.

As Christians and non-Christians talk about this matter of male and female roles, they often have very different presuppositions concerning matters which are fundamental to the whole argument. They have different assumptions about such things as what it is to be human, or what it is to be free and fulfilled as a person. These differing presuppositions can be so pervasive that people can even end up using the same words but meaning totally different things, and so talking almost completely at cross purposes. Hence we must begin by considering our assumptions. What are the Christian's presuppositions?

The human identity

The reality of the living God, the God and Father of our Lord Jesus Christ, the God of the Bible, is the primary Christian assumption. But this prime assumption provides us with the key to understanding what human beings, male and female, are.

1. The Christian believes in God as the Creator

That is so fundamental as to be non-negotiable. The very opening words of the Bible remind us: 'In the beginning God created...' Later we read, 'Let us make man...' The Scriptures constantly remind us of the absolute distinction between God and ourselves. He is the Creator and we are his creation. Our fundamental identity is that of creatures. Whatever views we might hold as to *how* God created (and this is not the place to go into that), we cannot but believe *that* God created. This is a bedrock assumption that must shape our thinking as Christians on every issue, including that of gender.

2. We are God's special creation

'Let us make man in our image.' As we read through Genesis 1, the chapter of creation, we find that this sentence is a new departure. During the days of creation God has made many things. But he has never before stood back from his creation and spoken to himself saying, 'Let us do this,' by way of reflecting, or premeditating, on what he is going to do. If you look back at God's previous creative acts (vv. 3,6,9,11,14,20,24), the pattern is simply God announcing, 'Let these be...', and then we read, 'And it was so.' It is almost as if previously God were creating by remote control. But when God comes to create man it is a vast new step. He stops to consider and declares, 'Let us make man.' It is as if human beings are the pinnacle for which everything else has been put in place, in readiness to receive them. God is personally involved as never before in an act of creation. Human beings are extraordinarily special in God's eyes. We are the objects of profound love from God.

3. We were made in the image of God, in the likeness of God (vv. 26,27)

What the invisible God is, infinitely and eternally, that human beings are visibly in time. So if God is wise, human beings have wisdom. Is God powerful? Then men and women are given power. Is God holy? Then that is reflected in the structure of the human personality. We have consciences. God is personal and spiritual. We are personal and spiritual too. There is dispute among theologians over precisely what the image of God in man means, but perhaps that is inevitable. Perhaps just as we can never fully understand or exhaust all that God is, for that very reason we can never fully delineate what it is to be made in God's image. Yes, it is to do with being persons and having a mind and conscience, but it is so much more. Everything we

are by creation reflects the nature of God. God is the only true
reference-point by which we can understand ourselves. Though
we share many qualities with the animal creation, being made
of the same dust, yet we find our identity upward in God, not
downward in the animals.

4. Our relationship to the rest of creation

Our greatness is also seen in our special calling, to rule the
world on behalf of God (vv. 26,28). The kind of rule envisaged
here is not a tyrannical dominance, but a rule of care and nurturing of the world. This finds particular expression in Adam's
work as the gardener of Eden (Gen. 2:15). We are to make the
earth fruitful and beautiful. Man stands between God and the
rest of creation as God's caring vicegerent. We are the crown of
creation.

5. The man and the woman, male and female, are equally made in God's image

Genesis 1:27 emphasizes that:

> In the image of God
>   he created him;
> male and female
>   he created them.

The man is no more the image of God than the woman is. That
is the implication here. Nowhere else is sexuality referred to in
the opening chapter of the Bible. But it is mentioned here. It is
important. The Bible is emphasizing that male and female are
equally God's image, equally valuable, and together they rule
over creation.

6. Both the man and the woman in Eden were accountable to God

This fact is of enormous importance. It is God who has made us. He is the one who defines us and commands us. He gave human beings immense freedom (Gen. 2:16). But he is the one who also warns of punishment for disobedience (Gen. 2:17). Both the man and the woman are questioned and held responsible for their part in the Fall (Gen. 3:11,13). We are, male and female, distinct from the dumb animal creation in this. We have a moral sense written into us. We are capable of recognizing the will of God and are held responsible for our choices with respect to it.

All these things listed here we have in common as men and women. Before we are either male or female, we are *human*. To be human is to be related to God in the ways we have described. We need to recognize and stress first of all that we have this common identity. To neglect that is disastrous. It is to make male and female two distinct species, which they are not. A very popular secular book on gender issues during the 1990s was *Men are from Mars, Women are from Venus* by John Grey. The book contains some good advice, but its tongue-in-cheek title gives the impression that ultimately men and women are alien to each other, that it is as if they originated from different planets. With such an assumption, if it was taken seriously, we would need to ask whether men and women were ever meant to relate to each other. We would have to face the question of whether the problems of relationships between the genders were actually insurmountable. But the biblical truth of our creation assures us that this is not the case. The identity of man and woman as made in the image of God, accountable to him and beloved by him, is the first of our fundamental presuppositions.

The human drama

Men and women have far more in common than they have differences. Scripture not only clarifies human identity; it also unfolds the human story. To be human, according to the Bible, also includes being caught up in a great drama. We share the story of creation, the fall into sin and redemption, which is offered to us in Christ. We do not understand ourselves unless we understand where we are located in the history of man's relationship to God.

1. Creation

We have noted this already, but it needs to be emphasized from another perspective. The point is that we are created beings and specifically *not* accidents of evolution. Neither were we brought into existence by some unknowable deity. The Christian assumption about men and women is that we are *planned* beings. Male and female are the *design* of God, and he has revealed himself and his plans to us in Scripture. Not only so, but because we are made in the image of God the Creator, the natural world is intelligible to us, and, indeed, is made for us as a home (Gen. 1:28-29; 2:19-20). This is immediately and markedly different from the secular presuppositions concerning men and women. In particular, gender difference is not fortuitous. It is not a product of chance. It is not something unreasonable and unintelligible. It is not something to be regretted, or to fight against. It is to be gratefully accepted as the good gift of a loving God. Both male and female have their creation in common.

2. Fall

But the human drama is such that we are no longer as God created us. Equally, as individual men and women, we have rebelled against God and are accountable for our sins. We have become hostile to our Creator, and unable to stand before his holiness. Since the first man and woman turned away from God there is now something desperately flawed about human nature. As men and women we have our sin in common. Once more we have to say that this is at loggerheads with many secular ideas. The secularist usually wants to speak of all men and women in such terms as, 'We're all good at heart.' There is a lot of good in people, for we were made in God's image. But it is not true that people are basically good. The Bible would say that we are inherently self-centred and sinful. To approach the troubles of contemporary men and women while ignoring the problem of sin is catastrophic. Sin is no small aberration. In the words of C. S. Lewis, 'We are not merely imperfect creatures who need to grow; we are rebels who need to lay down our arms.'

3. Redemption

But both men and women stand equally in need of, and are equally summoned to accept, God's redemption for us in the Lord Jesus Christ, who died for our sin at Calvary. Christ is risen from the dead and ascended to the right hand of God to give us his Holy Spirit, who is poured out on his 'sons and daughters ... even on my servants, both men and women,' as the prophet says in the Old Testament (Joel 2:28-29). Salvation knows no gender boundaries. Equally, eternal life is given to all who believe.

So once again, reviewing the human story, we see essential commonality between men and women. We share together in redemption from the Fall, which can be seen as restoring us in the image of our Creator (Col. 3:10).

Implications

Here, then, in both human identity and the human story, we have the basic presuppositions about men and women as human beings. We have not yet touched on gender distinctives, but we have sketched what we have in common.

These basic assumptions have wide-ranging implications for the debate concerning male and female. We do not have space to work out in detail all the ramifications, but we will pick up here a few very fundamental matters in the consideration of male and female and how they should relate.

In this whole gender debate there are three words which come up frequently. One word is *freedom*; another is *dignity*. Both of these relate to the third word, *justice*. We all want dignity and freedom. The call is for freedom and dignity for women, and rightly so.

Now, with Christian presuppositions, what do those words mean? What is freedom, real freedom? Is it indistinguishable from the secular view of freedom? If we hold these biblical presuppositions about what human beings are, then what is true dignity? And both those concepts must relate to the matter of justice, for justice can surely be said to include that which promotes true freedom and dignity for the individual.

These, then, are crucial matters in the debate. Let us look at them.

1. Freedom

Holding different presuppositions about human beings, the secularist and the Christian (and, indeed, anyone committed to any other world-view) will have different ideas of what it is to be truly free.

For the secularist non-Christian there is no life after death. All that exists is here and now. We only have one life. We must make the most of it. We must enjoy our brief stay on earth. Thus with this outlook ultimately freedom has to do with pursuing pleasure for oneself. It is to be able to do as you like, to make your own rules, to be answerable to no one but yourself, to break the rules if necessary. (Actually it is to wish to be in the place of God.) 'If I had enough money and enough courage, I could do whatever I wanted; then I would be really free.'

But Scripture tells us that such a view of freedom is a mirage. No such freedom exists. The world is not like that. The world does have rules that we have not made up — scientific laws not least. It rejects the idea that reality is an illusion — just a construct of our minds. Genesis 1 asserts the reality of creation before there were any human beings to perceive it. The world is governed by laws made by God and to ignore them will not lead to freedom. To ignore the maker's instructions on any product leads to disaster.

And mentioning the matter of ignoring the Maker's instructions leads us to consider the fact of sin. Again our Christian presuppositions about how sin has affected the human race will impinge on this subject of freedom. If human nature is perverse and fallen, we shall naturally tend to choose things which are against God, and therefore ultimately harmful to us. If freedom is defined as being able to choose to do whatever we want, but our choosing is itself flawed, doesn't that leave our whole concept of freedom in ruins? Remember the title of Martin Luther's great book, *The Bondage of the Will.*

True freedom is not about doing whatever pleases us. A simple consideration from everyday life illustrates this. In Britain we drive our cars on the left-hand side of the road. If we all keep to that rule everything is generally fine; we are free to proceed to whatever destination we wish. But were people to abandon that rule and drive on the left or on the right according to their whim it would bring head-on collisions, chaos, death and tragedy — not freedom.

For the Christian the idea that freedom is to be able to 'do whatever you want' is an impossible view. Indeed it was rebellion against God's rule in Eden, with Adam taking the view, 'I'm going to do what I decide regardless of what God says,' which led, not to freedom, but to bondage and death.

True freedom is not lawless independence from God. Scripture says that true freedom is the freedom of obedient children. It is the freedom of children who love their Father (God) and whose Father loves them and, for their own good, has defined the area of choice open to them within definite limits. Here is freedom to enjoy themselves within a protected area. They use all their God-given powers of creativity to explore that area and use it to serve that Father whom they love, and in that they find great fulfilment. This is why, for example, God's Ten Commandments have so many 'You shall not…'s in them. God is setting out the boundary. 'Do not go beyond this line,' is the message for our own good. But, within the boundary God has marked out, we can safely use all our powers of self-expression under the smile of God. Here is true freedom. Here is true blessing and fulfilment.

All through Scripture freedom is seen in this light. It is never the 'no-limits', 'do-as-I-like' vision of secular culture. Think of the Exodus. God's people are in bondage in Egypt and through Moses God brings them out. He sets them free from their fetters, but what does he do? Does the Lord then say to them, 'Well, off you go! I am leaving you now. You can do as you like. Goodbye'? No, because he knows that would wreck them. They are sinners. Left to themselves they would run into more trouble. Rather he brings them out of Egypt and says to them, 'I have borne you on eagles' wings and brought you to myself that you might serve me and that I might bless you' (Exod. 19:4-5, paraphrase). They are brought into covenant relationship to God, for only in God's presence and in God's service is real freedom.

Think about what the Lord Jesus Christ said: 'You will know the truth, and the truth will set you free' (John 8:32). Postmodern individuals often say in effect, 'There is no such thing as truth. We want to make our own truth. I want to decide what is right and what is wrong for me.' That is especially the case in issues surrounding gender and male and female roles. But Jesus speaks, not of our making our own truth, but of our listening to his truth. It is Christ who is the way, the truth and the life (John 14:6).

The apostle Paul put the same truth in another way. Describing Christian conversion he wrote, 'You were slaves of sin but now you have become servants of righteousness' (Rom. 6:19-22, paraphrase). Paul is spelling out quite categorically that true freedom is inextricably bound up with righteousness. That is real freedom. Therefore, the Christian seeking true freedom for us all must ask what is righteous behaviour with respect to gender questions. It is God's command, God's service, which leads to freedom, so what has God said about the roles of male and female? True freedom can never be found in the overthrow of biblical norms of behaviour. It is because we are for freedom that we must go to our Bibles.

2. Dignity

As both men and women, we want dignity, and that is absolutely right. We want to be valued, to feel that we are worthwhile, and that is what God desires too for every human being. Bearing in mind the biblical presuppositions concerning what it is to be human, we now ask, 'How is true dignity to be found?'

Our secular society, having rejected God and biblical presuppositions, has a view of how dignity comes to human beings which is very different from the Christian outlook. And this view itself leads to many of the difficulties which arise over matters of gender.

Without God, we naturally turn to achievement as the way to acquire dignity. We must pursue 'respect' and 'street cred' from others. We must pursue business, artistic or sporting achievements. We are all performers and the rest of the world is our audience. We must make them take notice of us. Then we shall have dignity. Sadly, in the marketplace and the scramble of the Western world, it means that the achievement of human beings is measured by the materialistic standard. How much does she earn? How big is his house? How far is a person up the ladder in the corporation? If you have a big balance at the bank, or if you are a famous name or an influential person, then you have dignity. That is how the world works. Of course, with this scale of values, the traditional mother at home feels worthless and trapped. No wonder women have risen up in their frustration. Men thrust and tread on women and on each other in the battle to be a somebody.

But Scripture's view of dignity is at a vast distance from all this. First of all, the audience which views our lives and whose judgement matters, is not other people, but God. True dignity comes not from the acclaim of mankind, but from the smile and approval of God. The Lord Jesus was not so concerned about what the crowds thought of him, but he was blessed to hear the voice of his heavenly Father declaring, 'You are my Son, whom I love; with you I am well pleased' (Mark 1:11).

Secondly, the materialistic scale of values by which the world does its measuring of people means nothing in the eyes of God. God's values are about character rather than plaudits and being a 'personality'. The things the secular world is battling for are of no eternal worth. Paul tells us that what is seen is temporary, but what is unseen is eternal (2 Cor. 4:18).

I was in an office some time ago, during a time of economic downturn, where some wit had pinned up a notice which said, 'Due to the recession the light at the end of the tunnel has been turned off.' But that is a parody of secular life. We can imagine people scrambling through life towards the goal they want to achieve. They battle and strive so that they will arrive and bask in the light at the end of their tunnel and say, 'Everyone can see me now. I have achieved my aim.' But the light is going to be turned off, isn't it? Wealth and power may be all very well, but then death comes and these things mean nothing at all, and perhaps worse than nothing. Someone has rather bluntly said, 'When you have won the rat race you are still only a rat!' Where is the dignity in that?

But where do the Christian presuppositions lead us when we think of dignity? We are made in God's image. There is dignity to begin with. But we have turned from God. It is sin which defiles and defaces God's image. It is sin which takes away true dignity. But as we trust in Christ, who died for us, we are redeemed and we come into a living relationship with God, and the image of God is restored (Eph. 4:24). To be loved by God; to be known by him; to be like him; to be personally linked to his absoluteness for ever — that is real dignity! That is true significance.

And within that relationship with God there is the proper theatre for our life's achievement. We are to be achievers, but achievers for God. Having dismissed the rat race of this world, God does not encourage the Christian to drop out. We are not to be some sort of plankton that just drifts through life doing nothing. God has made us in his image with many powers and abilities. These are to be used, not for self-aggrandizement, but for the eternal glory of God. We should rightly desire dignity for all men and women. So when we ask about genuine dignity the Christian is driven back to God.

3. Justice

The idea of justice is one that emerges repeatedly in the debate about the roles of men and women in society and in the church. But once again we have to recognize that justice is a word the meaning of which will vary with our presuppositions. It is only once we have got our ideas concerning freedom and dignity clarified from a biblical standpoint that we are in a proper position to construct a correct view of justice. As human beings, with freedom of choice within the limits imposed by God, we are accountable for our actions. Justice is ultimately to do with what is right or wrong in God's sight. Justice is to do with treating people fairly — that is, in accordance with what they are as free and dignified, but fallen, individuals, answerable to their Creator. In particular, within a biblical framework justice is not simply about relationships between human beings; it must incorporate the question of how I as an individual, male or female, am relating to the God who made me.

As Christians we have to see freedom, dignity and justice from this totally different perspective. We have to start there. We Christians are in a different kingdom from this world. We are part of the kingdom of God. This world looks at it and thinks it is an upside-down kingdom. It is a kingdom in which dependence brings freedom. It is a kingdom in which servanthood means dignity. But it is the kingdom of God. We need to look at this whole matter of male and female roles with that kind of perspective. If you are a man it will challenge you. If you are a woman it will challenge you too. It is from the perspective of 'What has God made me as a man, or me as a woman, to be?'

Now that brings us to a challenge. The challenge is the challenge of personal submission to God. How is freedom found, true freedom? In personal submission to God. What is true dignity? To be a servant of the Lord, who came among us as one who served (Luke 22:27); to live freely and creatively within the loving plan of our Creator. Therein lies a just and fair way of life. Therein lies our salvation. It is through the surrender of faith in Jesus as Lord that we become Christians. What is the status of your personal submission to God and mine?

Let me quote from Jim Packer: 'Man's lie is that our dignity forbids us to serve either God or our fellow human beings though (in the worst case) it requires them to serve us.' In other words, on the secular view our 'dignity' justifies our egoism. But God's truth is that our dignity is only realized as we love and serve God for himself and love mankind and serve mankind for God's sake. Packer goes on: 'The alternative is to demean and dehumanize ourselves.'[1]

God has made us royalty in his world, for he is the great King. Just as great princes or great princesses display their dignity, and do not forfeit their dignity or their nobility, by making obeisance to the sovereign, so we mortal men wear our dignity most clearly and plainly as we submit to the King, as we live lives of worship to the Most High.

What is the status of your submission to God? That is where humanity and true dignity are found. That is where salvation and life are found — in surrendering to Jesus Christ. That, too, is where the key to true masculinity and true femininity is found.

Questions

1. Summarize in a few sentences the main assumptions which Bible-believing Christians bring to considering gender issues.
2. List some of the logical differences you see between a Christian view of freedom and an atheistic view of freedom (see, for example, Gal. 5:13).
3. How does the example of Jesus make a Christian view of freedom differ from that of someone who only believes in a Creator but not in the incarnation and life of Christ? (Consider for example, Mark 10:45; Luke 22:27).
4. Spend some time quietly meditating on the great dignity of being a human being, made in God's image. Turn that meditation into a prayer of praise. Now read James 3:9-10.

1. J. I. Packer & Thomas Howard, *Christianity: The True Humanism,* Word Publishing, Waco, 1985.

2.

Man according to the Bible

Genesis 2:4-25

Women tend to have two complaints about men. ('Only two?' you say!) 'I wouldn't go out with him,' they say. 'He's such a wimp!' That's one. 'I can't stand him. He's such a chauvinist, always trying to push women around!' That's the other. There is something to be deduced from those remarks. They indicate what women are looking for in a man. Although opposite observations, they focus on the same area of a man's personality. Women feel that true manliness has something to do with this area of strength of character, and the trouble is that as men we tend to shoot either side of the mark. Either we are too wet and weak, or we are too self-engrossed and assertive, too much of the bully-boy.

One of our basic presuppositions, as we have seen, in approaching masculinity and femininity is that male and female are not accidents of nature. God planned and designed us. Therefore we need to hear what God our Maker has to say on the subject of gender. The scheme in this chapter is to sketch out from the Bible the idea of masculinity as God intended it to be. In the next chapter we will look similarly at femininity.

There are great tensions in our society at the moment over how men and women are to relate. Tensions are brought into marriage, church and business, and all kinds of problems arise.

Therefore we need to submit our minds to God's Word. What does God say about what it is to be male? What women instinctively feel about what a man ought to be is that masculinity centres around a certain type of strength of character. Hence the opening comments of this chapter. We shall see that they are basically right. Don't get me wrong; you can have women with a strength of character as well. But there is a real sense in which there is a different slant that makes for manliness. I think women perceive that. So we look at the question of masculinity.

Why is this subject important?

It is an important subject for all kinds of reasons, but we shall consider three in this chapter.

1. Psychologically

It is important because, in the words of the Christian writer Elizabeth Elliot, 'It's dangerous and destructive to treat sexuality as if it were meaningless. Much of the church, which is being strongly influenced by the world's ideologies, is ignoring the fact that sexuality means something.'

Many people want to play down gender differences as if they do not mean much. But that is not true. First of all, we are all human, but we are all either male or female, and that maleness and femaleness are the design of God and go right to the root of what we are as persons. 'God created man … male and female he created them' (Gen. 1:27). To make out that gender is not a very significant factor really entails a kind of shutting down, or a glossing over, of a vast area of our personalities as God made us. To do that will distort us and harm us. Our masculinity (or femininity) is a deep part of us. What is it? Is it just a matter of physical differences — or is there much more to it than that? We need to know. So that is the first reason why this question is important.

2. In the family

It is important to our children. All of us, of course, begin our lives inside our mother's womb. We are part of her, joined to her by the umbilical cord even as we are born. The child clings close to its mother in early years, and the establishment of our own separate identity, independent of our parents, is a very important part of growing to maturity.

Psychologists tell us that the father (the parent to whom the child has never been physically attached as with the mother) plays a big part in helping both girls and boys develop as separate personalities. Fathers, in particular, help us to mature as people. An old proverb puts it like this: 'A man is never a man until his father tells him he is a man.' There is a lot of wisdom in that. The first nine chapters of the Bible's book of Proverbs are the teaching of a father to his son, seeking to lead him to maturity (cf. Prov. 3:1-4; Luke 2:52).

Think about it: 'A man is never a man until his father tells him he is a man.' It is not just the sentence, 'You are a man,' that needs to be said. Fathers communicate to their children by the whole way they interact with them. To their sons they must communicate the message: 'Yes, I am now looking at you as another man, the same as me.'

Research seems to show that the roots of distorted male personalities and homosexual tendencies are often linked to a failure of relationship between father and son. The father has failed to affirm his son's masculinity. Fathers with no true strength of character bring problems into their family here. Perhaps they are fathers who have been knocked about by life in their careers, but have vented their anger about that by being violent in the family, treating wife and children with disrespect. Perhaps they have reacted by withdrawing into themselves, becoming non-communicative, frequently shutting themselves away from the family in their study or their computer-room, avoiding any genuine relationship with their children. These are fathers who perhaps deserve sympathy, but who have failed to be strong enough to rise above their own problems and forget themselves in order to have a proper fatherly relationship with their children. Our children need fathers who are 'men'. But what is it to be a man? We need to answer that question.

This matter of a father's relationship to his children has been given even greater importance by the work of Professor Paul Vitz of New York University. In 1999 he published a book[1] in which he brings a great deal of evidence to suggest that atheism is linked to absent or malfunctioning fathers. Reading the biographies of many of the most famous atheists in history led him to this conclusion. A bad relationship, or a non-existent relationship, with a father can often lead to a wish to do away with the idea of God, the great Father. This applies in different ways to both male and female children. This is not the place to go into this fully, but if what Vitz says holds water then once again we see the importance of a loving, biblical masculinity in the leadership of the Christian family. Further we see that the contemporary attack on the family is actually a spiritual battle with far-reaching consequences.

3. Individual Christian growth

All Christian men need to have a clear picture of manhood, in order to keep in step with the Holy Spirit in growing, as Christians, into what we ought to be. It is true that most aspects of Christian character and growth are common to both men and women. The whole matters of love, faith and hope are common to us all. But if you read your New Testament in detail, you do find clear gender-specific instructions. For example, in Titus 2 Paul goes through a list saying, 'Teach the older men to be temperate ... teach the older women to be reverent...' and then he goes on and tells Titus to teach the younger women something else and to 'encourage the young men to be self-controlled'. There is teaching that is specific to male and female (see also 1 Timothy; 1 Peter 5 and 1 John 2). We need to take that on board. Men and women are in some ways different from one another and therefore in need of particular slants of the application of the gospel. We need to acknowledge these things in order that we can be led by the Holy Spirit as he goes about making us all that he would have us be.

So why are these things important? For the health of our own personality, for our children and for our Christian growth, this is an important issue. It is important especially in these days when we are under so much pressure from a world that has taken on a secular, very anti-God ideology which it actively promotes all the time.

What is a man?

The Bible is full of what it is to be a man, and full of what a woman is as well. We take up the matter of masculinity briefly from Genesis 2. We are speaking of Genesis chapter 2, which, as I hope you have noticed, comes before Genesis 3! In other words, what we are looking at occurs *before* the Fall. So we are looking at the situation where sin has not distorted either us or our world. Genesis 2 shows us things as God intended them to be. Here, then, we are shown patterns that we may not achieve perfectly in a fallen world, but to which we can aspire in Christ. Here is something of a God-given blueprint on which we can safely base our ideas. The narrative emphasizes two things as we ask this question: 'What is a man?'

1. Man is the same as the woman!

The first emphasis from Genesis 2 is that the man is precisely the same as the woman. We need to remind ourselves of this again; otherwise the rest of what is said will be out of balance. Unless we begin here it will look as if what I have to say about the differences is everything, but it is not. It needs to be seen in the context of all that we have in common.

Now how do we see that man and woman are the same? Look first of all at Genesis 2:18. Here is God's great work. Having said repeatedly about creation in Genesis 1 that 'It is very good', God makes this startling statement that it is *not* good for man to be alone. That is a shock: 'It is not good for the man to be alone. I will make a helper suitable for him.'

What follows on from that? The next incident of which we read is Adam's naming of the animals. They are brought to Adam as the ruler and he expresses his authority over the animal kingdom by naming them. 'But for Adam no suitable helper was found' (v. 20). They are different from man and they will not do as close companions. I know we have the saying about a dog being a man's best friend, but a dumb animal can never fulfil the human potential for relationships.

What happens next? We read in verses 21-22, 'So the LORD God caused the man to fall into a deep sleep; and while he was sleeping, he took one of the man's ribs ["rib" is actually a more general word meaning half of the man's side] and closed up the place with flesh. Then the LORD God made a woman from the rib he had taken out of the man, and he brought her to the man.' God makes woman, not simply out of the ground, as he made Adam. He does not just make Eve of the same substance, but from *the very same body* as Adam. There could not be a better way of showing identity. She is the same as Adam, precisely the same.

Then what happens? Adam awakes. God brings the woman to him and, not only is the woman made the same as him, but Adam *recognizes* that fact. He verifies her identity with him. In verse 23 we have the first piece of human poetry. That is why the text is set out differently from the surrounding words in modern Bible versions. Adam sees this wonderful woman; he is delighted; his heart leaps and he says:

> This is now bone of my bones
>   and flesh of my flesh;
> she shall be called 'woman',
>   for she was taken out of man.

He declares, 'She's the *same* as me!' The poetry and the words express his feelings and demonstrate that he is thrilled!

At the end of verse 23 in the Hebrew we read, 'She shall be called "Isshah", for she was taken out of "Ish".' Those original words sound so much the same and thus again indicate the closeness of male and female. That word-play is partly preserved with the words 'woman' and 'man' that we use. They emphasize the unity between us. This links back with Genesis 1:27, where male and female are both created by the Lord, both made in the image of God.

'What is man?' The first answer to that question which we must not miss is: 'The same as woman!' We are partners. We never read in Scripture that a man is worth more than a woman. Never in Scripture do we read that men are naturally more intelligent than women. One is not better than the other. Men who forget this are desperately wrong. Women who forget this are desperately wrong too. We are the same. That is the first emphasis in Genesis 2. But now we turn to the second answer to the question: 'What is a man?'

2. Man is different from the woman!

Now we can begin to identify what are biblical distinguishing features of the male. I want to emphasize that what we have here in Genesis 2 is not a stereotype. Stereotypes arise from social conditioning. But what we are confronted with here, if we believe the Bible is God's Word, are not stereotypes but God's archetypes of male and female. They are the original models, or patterns, from which the others flow. This is not a matter of social conditioning; this is a matter of God's creation.

If we return to Genesis 2:18 we read God saying, 'I will make a helper suitable for him.' The word translated 'suitable' is literally 'opposite' him. Out of the same flesh and blood, God made someone who was 'other' than man, in a real sense 'opposite' to man. The two are the same and yet opposite — different. How can that be?

Did you attend chemistry lessons at school? If you did you will perhaps remember allotropes. These are natural occurrences of the very same substance in more than one form. So you can have charcoal and diamonds, which are allotropes of the element carbon. Or you can have different allotropes of sulphur — crystalline and non-crystalline. They are precisely the same substance, but they are different in form and structure. That is an illustration we can think about when it comes to males and females. It is almost as if we can say that man and woman are allotropes of one another. They are the same and yet they are opposite.

What are the distinctives of man here? There are at least three, moving through Genesis 2.

Work

The first word that gives a clue as to what is particular to the man here is 'work'. God made the man, according to Genesis 2, for a purpose, and made him to suit that purpose (Gen.

2:5,8,15). Man was put in the garden to 'work'. Please don't rush to the conclusion that I am saying that women don't work, or shouldn't work. But this is the distinctive of the male. This matter of work is the first thing that is obviously peculiar to Adam here. Archetypal man is a worker, one who is involved in tasks.

I can remember, many years ago now, there was an experiment shown on the BBC TV *Horizon* programme. Psychologists did some experiments with children, and the children were told that they were going to do a test. The children had to wait in a room together in small groups before they went through to do their test. But, unbeknown to them, the real experiment was the camera focusing on them in the room before they went into this test. There in the room were play bricks and they filmed how pairs of children reacted to being left in this room together with these bricks and before they went in to do their test. They found a very distinct difference. The boys talked together particularly about the task: 'What are we going to do with these bricks? How are we going to do it?' The girls were rather different. They tended to talk more about one another. They got on with the task but their conversation included such things as, 'How many dollies have you got at home?' 'What is your room like?' They wanted to know about one another, whereas the boys weren't particularly interested to know about one another. They were talking about the task. That fits very much with what we have here in Genesis 2. That distinctive is not by chance. It goes right back to Genesis. The man is the worker.

Work means a great deal to men. Writing in the *Guardian* newspaper in 1987, during a time of economic recession in Britain when many men were out of work, Tim Kemp, a training consultant, said, 'Men use work in the same way we use clothing. It is not just status we are looking for; it's an identity. We invest everything in our work. Without it men feel they have lost their place in the world — they have become non-people ... men view life without a job as meaningless.'

The focus of the female's task is rather different and we shall take that up later. Of course, this matter of work for men is underlined in the New Testament. In 2 Thessalonians 3:10 the apostle Paul writes, 'If a man will not work, he shall not eat.' If he is a loafer — not out of work or unable to work through disability, but someone who will not work, who is idle — he is denying the faith, says the apostle Paul. A man like that is going against what it is to be a man, refusing to work and get on. Again, with working for a living in mind, Paul says that 'If anyone does not provide for his relatives, and especially for his immediate family, he has denied the faith and is worse than an unbeliever' (1 Tim. 5:8). The Lord Jesus Christ, our Saviour, spent years working in the carpenter's shop (Mark 6:3). The Son of God himself has set men an example of honest toil. Men particularly are made for work.

For that very same reason redundancy and unemployment are such a blow to good men. Being out of work has such a great impact on them because they know it is a very deep part of their personality to be workers. This question of work is reflected in the way God made men physically. Men, generally speaking, are made physically *stronger* than women. There is the muscle structure of the male. Men are usually bigger and more muscular in the upper body, and again the New Testament takes that up when Peter says, 'Be considerate as you live with your wives ... the weaker partner' (1 Peter 3:7). Peter is not saying that women are intellectually weak, or anything like that, but is just stating what is plainly obvious, that men, generally speaking, are physically stronger people.

Thus, traditionally and biblically, the male has been the so-called bread-winner in a family. A question might be raised here. With the advent of industrialization, and especially the development of the computer, work is no longer such a physical pursuit. Does this advance in technology make a difference to the link between men and work?

We have to say that work-patterns have indeed changed. However, the psychological need for men to achieve and provide through work is still very much there. Also, although much work may have changed from being manual to being more cerebral, still manual labour is often required in industries and such tasks as mending or building roads. And even with more cerebral occupations, very often the pressures of the modern workplace, frequently coupled with the exhausting and frustrating business of commuting to and from work, still require a good deal of physical strength. God made men in particular that way to fit in with this matter of work. (The arduous regime of the modern workplace can place many pressures on families. For a discussion of some of the factors involved see Appendix III at the end of the book.)

Initiative/Leadership

Male and female together are royalty, God's regents on earth. Together we are the rulers of the world. Genesis 1:26,28 implies this: 'Let them rule over the fish of the sea…' — together. 'God blessed *them* and said to *them*, " Be fruitful … Rule over …' (emphasis added). But the initiative, the ground-breaking aspect of that rule, lays with the male.

How do I know that? First of all, because the man was made first. That was not because the male is somehow better than the female, but simply to reflect this aspect of his character. Man is to be the pioneer. So here in Genesis 2, where we focus in more specifically on how God made male and female, the male is made first. This cannot be dismissed as an irrelevant detail of the creation story. The apostle Paul picks it up in 1 Timothy 2:13, and uses it to reflect on how men and women ought to relate to one another in the sight of God.

I have heard an argument that says, 'Weren't the sea monsters made before the man? So wouldn't that mean that somehow monsters must lead men?' implying that the deduction from the order of creation is invalid. That is nonsense. The animals are a completely different aspect of creation. It is the male and the female who are the rulers. We are on a different level from the beasts. But within that royal family that God has put here on the earth, the man is made first. He is the one who makes those first acts of rulership over the creation. He tills and cares for the Garden of Eden before Eve is ever made. He categorizes the beasts and names the animals. Again, when Eve is presented to Adam in all her feminine glory, Adam takes the initiative and speaks about this and gives her the name 'woman'. And the comment of Genesis 2:24 reflects male initiative: 'For this reason *a man will leave* his father and mother and be united to his wife' (emphasis added). It picks up the male initiative in pursuing the woman.

Male initiative is reflected in our physical make-up. Think about procreation. The male implants the seed. The female receives the male sperm. It is the male who initiates the life within the womb. Or think about some of the complaints that now and again come across from women about men: 'I wish he would make a decision.' 'He always wants me to make the first move.' Isn't that what women often say? 'I wish he would take the initiative.' 'I wish he would be the man that he ought to be.' Women are unhappy when their men do not seem to have any enterprise.

We will explore the idea of male initiative and leadership further in a later chapter.

Sacrifice

This is the third word which characterizes the male. Let us notice again Genesis 2:18. God declares, 'It is not good for the man to be alone. I will make a helper suitable for him.' Adam

alone is unfulfilled; he is incomplete. He is made for a relationship with another human being. Just as he is in a relationship
with God, and as God is in relationship with himself in the
persons of the Trinity, so man is made for relationship with
someone who is his equal (and, of course, so is woman). How
does that relationship come about? How is Eve, that other person, created? How does Adam find that missing someone in
his life and find fulfilment? Genesis 2:20-21 tells us it was by
giving of himself.

The man allows God to take something from him. He allows himself to be diminished. He sacrifices part of himself:
'Then the LORD God made a woman from the rib he had taken
out of the man.' It is as the man makes this sacrifice that he
finds all that he has always desired. Adam's response is: 'This is
now bone of my bones and flesh of my flesh' (v. 23). Again we
can relate that back to the physical way God has made men.
God made men with the strength to make sacrifices for the
'making' of others. That is true manliness. Male strength is
wrongly and sinfully misused when it is used to dominate. Male
strength is given for service and brave deeds. It is not meant for
selfishness or domination. It is precisely this aspect of courageous
sacrifice which Paul has in mind when he encourages the
Corinthian Christian to 'play the man' (1 Cor. 16:13, Greek).

This aspect of sacrifice is again not a mere incidental of the
Genesis account. Just as Christ obtained his bride, the church,
through sacrificing himself (Eph. 5:25), so Adam obtained Eve
through sacrificially giving of himself.

All of these distinguishing features of the male must, of course,
be seen in the context of obedience. As human beings, we are
all responsible to God. In Eden all we have seen of Adam has
been in co-operation with, and obedience to, God. Without
that word 'obedience' undergirding everything, we are going to
end up with a badly distorted view of manliness. So we can

already see that the Hollywood version of masculinity is frequently very unhelpful. The modern Arnold Schwarzenegger or Bruce Willis image of manliness as power to dominate is a perversion of the biblical concept, for it does not link strength to obedience.

Work, initiative and sacrifice — these, together, form the male distinctive. We must say at this point that we must take these things relatively. It is not that women do not work, or take initiative, or sacrifice. They do. We are the same. But in the male these things have particular prominence. Women have their own distinctives, as we shall see in the next chapter. But for the male these things are the centre of the orbit. God did not make a unisex being. He made men and women and they are different. Further, we must take this focus relatively because we must allow for different personalities. Not all men are the same, or meant to be the same. We have different characteristics. Some are naturally extroverts, others more quiet. Some enjoy physical pursuits; others are more intellectual or artistic. But wherever the location of our personality, whatever character direction we come from, as men in our own way, we are to aim at being sacrificial workers for the good of others. I hope that by now we have at least some idea of what it is to be a man.

The word 'initiative' could be linked to the word 'leadership'. But I am unhappy about that word in some respects because it has been so debased by modern ideas of managers who 'sit up there and make decisions' and have nothing to do with what is happening 'on the ground'. It has been devalued too by generals who have 'led' by sending their troops into battle from the safe distance of a headquarters situated twenty miles behind the front line! That has nothing to do with biblical leadership. Biblical leadership is more to do with the idea of a pioneer — a person who says, 'I go *first*, to take the risks, to make the way safe for others, to take the knocks.'

Summarizing man

So we have a definition of maleness, from what we have seen, that could go something like this:

> Masculinity is that deep sense of responsibility to lead in a strong and self-sacrificial way, to work for the glory of God and the good of others.

I use that word 'sense' because some good men are elderly or disabled and I don't want them to think they are not men because they can't get on and do what they want to do. But it is the *sense* of responsibility in that area that is true masculinity.

Another remark I must make is that God does reveal himself in male terms. He calls himself 'he'. He uses words like 'king', instead of 'queen', and 'master', instead of 'mistress', in describing himself in Scripture. We are to be balanced about this, but we must recognize this and pursue a theology which is comfortable with the fact that God reveals himself almost exclusively in male terms. That is not to say that somehow the male is more in God's image than the woman. We shall see why later. But God does reveal himself in male terms.

Why? Because he is the great worker, the one with almighty power in creation and redemption. He is the one who takes the initiative. When we were in sin he took the initiative of grace. He decided; he acted; he came. He is the one, of course, who made the great sacrifice. Christ came as a man and went to the cross for us. With all his strength, Jesus resists the temptation to run away. Here he is giving of himself, taking the initiative of love, paying the price. Here is our role-model — Jesus. We are the bride, he the husband. C. S. Lewis puts it like this: 'God is so masculine that all creation (men and woman) are feminine by contrast.' God is so masculine in his work, in his power, in his sacrifice that the church, composed of both sexes, cannot be described in any other way than as the bride.

Application

Perhaps some male readers may be thinking, 'How can I be a man?' The answer is that there is no way you will be a true man without being with God. The only true men, fully as they ought to be, were Adam — before the Fall — and Jesus Christ. How will you be the man that you ought to be? You will not be unless you are with God. When Adam walked out on God in Eden he fell in his masculinity. We need the Lord himself in our lives to be the men we ought to be, to give us the strength that we need to be the kind of loving, wise, sacrificial men that God would have us to be. There is a need for repentance. Perhaps single men have used the strength that they have to serve themselves rather than other people. Perhaps husbands have used their strength to dominate their wives and children. We need to come back to God, back to his Word of Scripture, and learn again to walk with him. To be a loving sacrificial servant of others, as Jesus Christ was, is not to be namby-pamby. It is to be a true man.

Questions

1. From Genesis chapters 1 and 2, in what ways are men and women the same?
2. In the light of what we have seen of what ought to characterize maleness, take time to read through 1 Samuel chapters 17-31. Contrast and compare the lives of David and Saul. List examples to follow, and others to avoid.
3. This chapter argues that the male emphasis is to do with work, initiative and sacrifice. If you are a man, think through your own

personality and life situation and decide on practical ways in which you could be more manly in the biblical sense.

4. Are there other emphases which you think ought to be included to give a more rounded view of biblical manliness, which have not been mentioned in this chapter?

1. Paul Vitz, *Faith of the Fatherless,* Spence Publishing Co., Dallas, 1999.

3.
Woman according to the Bible

Genesis 2:4-25

Have you ever been to see that rather delightful musical *My Fair Lady*? It is both a stage show and a classic film. The story is about Professor Higgins, who takes the London cockney flower girl Eliza and seeks to make her into a well-spoken, stylish lady. It is a charming tale and of course he ends up falling in love with her. It is based on George Bernard Shaw's play *Pygmalion*. Through the tortuous speech training their relationship knows many ups and downs and Professor Higgins asks in one of the songs, 'Why can't a woman be more like a man?' and he goes on:

> Men are so pleasant,
> So easy to please,
> Whenever you're with them
> You're always at ease.

Then he turns to his compatriot, Colonel Pickering and says, 'Would you be slighted if I didn't speak for hours?'
'No', says Pickering.
'Would you be livid if I'd had a drink or two?'
'Certainly not'.
'Would you be wounded if I never sent you flowers?'

'No, never.'
'Well, why can't a woman be like you?'

Why can't a woman be like a man? Our times are seriously
answering, 'Indeed, why not?' A great tide seeking to diminish,
or even to exclude completely, distinctions between male and
female has swept through our society. I am sure some of the
changes have been helpful. But as Christians we want to assess
these things in the light of Scripture.

As was pointed out at the beginning, the starting-point of
the Bible is creation. Male and female are not accidents that
just happen to have arisen by chance. They are the design of
God. That is firmly there in the first chapters of Genesis:

> So God created man
>   in his own image,
> in the image of God
>   he created him;
> male and female
>   he created them
>
> (Gen. 1:27).

Male and female are different and to try to insist there is no real
difference, apart from a few bits of biology, is unwise. In the
long run it could be highly destructive. Our brief now, therefore,
is to seek to identify from the Bible the main ideas of femininity
as God intended it to be.

We go back again to Genesis 2, before the entrance of sin
into the world. Even Professor Higgins had to acknowledge
there is a difference. The very question, 'Why can't a woman
be like a man?' implies it. Well, what is the difference? We are
going to use the same structure as in the previous chapter on
masculinity. So we begin with the same question, though this
time we look at what it is to be feminine.

Why is this subject so important?

1. It is important to women personally

Women today are constantly bombarded with false ideas of femininity. There are basically two alternatives.

First of all, the media and advertising world, still very much male-dominated, would promote the vision of the female as the dumb blonde. Here femininity is that of a simpering kind of woman with her eyes ever widening, enthralled by her macho man. It is all about eyelashes and high heels. It is to be a 'living doll' with which men can play. That is one vision of femininity.

On the other hand, the feminist lobby would urge women to go to the other extreme. As opposed to the first alternative, where the woman is so keen to be attractive to men, the feminist lobby would say, 'No, no, don't even bother about that. Rather be a contender with men. Be aggressive, be assertive, be out there, taking men on. Don't focus on the family. That is to be a failure as a woman. Be independent.' That is the other vision.

Neither of these two is the biblical view. These are caricatures of true womanhood. And, that being the case, to pursue either of those avenues will not bring fulfilment as a woman. We have to say that the first model, that of the 'living doll', is unhelpful. Feminism itself is partly a reaction by women who felt imprisoned in that very kind of caricature. It does not work for women.

Take the other model of aggressively trying to eliminate all differences between men and women. This experiment has been tried many times before and it has not brought happiness to women. One of the experiments that took this up was that of the kibbutz system in Israel. After the Second World War the kibbutz system was set up in the newly found state of Israel. These were communities where men and women lived and worked together — and it set out to do away with sex-roles. The ordinary nuclear family in some of these communities was eliminated. But half a century later, that kibbutz system has dwindled. Why did it decline? I understand it was largely the women who got rid of it. They led the way back to demanding more time with their children and back to insisting that they wanted particular roles within the home. The 'Women are the same as men' system didn't satisfy them.

Similar evidence came from a BBC TV *Panorama* programme in January 2000, at the turn of the new millennium. Research was carried out into the lives of 560 mothers in Britain who had started full-time jobs. After two years of such work, one third of the women had left. About half of those who left had gone into part-time work and the other half had left the workplace altogether. They wanted more time to be with their children. The impression was given that many of those who had stayed in full-time employment wished that they did not have to do so. They were dissatisfied and felt upset, especially if they had to leave their children with child-minders. Making no distinction between men and women is a flawed idea.

These brief pieces of evidence indicate the importance of this question of 'What is femininity?' It seems the secular visions of femininity frequently do not lead to fulfilment for women as persons. It is important because caricatures lead to disillusion.

2. *It is important to society*

It is historically true that one of the foundations of stable and healthy society is the influence of good women. I came across something that Mikhail Gorbachev, the former leader of the Soviet Union, said in 1987. In the old USSR this matter of seeking to play down the differences between male and female was part of the original revolution of 1917. The Communist experiment failed. But this is one of the things that Gorbachev said: 'We have discovered that many of our problems — in children's and young people's behaviour, in our morals, culture and in production — are particularly caused by the weakening of family ties and slack attitude to family responsibilities. This is a paradoxical result of our sincere desire to make women as much the same as men in everything.'

Isn't that strange? He is in effect saying, 'Look, we have set out in this direction with sincere hearts, wanting to do good and yet it led in the wrong direction. It hasn't worked.' The fabric of society is undermined if we are not careful when we play around. The Christian realizes that such things are bound to happen, for we are tampering with something fundamental which God has put there from the beginning. Family roles are not accidents. Male and female were planned. The feminine has vast power for good in society, but we need to be clear as to what it is to be feminine.

Much more could be said, but those are my two reasons for saying that it is important. It is important personally and important for society.

What is a woman?

As in the previous chapter, we will focus on Genesis 2 but also draw upon other scriptures. What answer does Scripture give to this question: 'What is it to be female? What is a woman?' I am purposely repeating many things that were said previously so that the balance is maintained within this crucial chapter. The first answer that Genesis 2 gives to our question is, of course, the point from which we started in the previous chapter.

1. Woman is the same as the man

We need to underline that, lest we get things in the wrong perspective. The whole emphasis is that man and woman are precisely the same. Look again at verse 21: 'So the LORD God caused the man to fall into a deep sleep; and while he was sleeping, he took one of the man's ribs and closed up the place with flesh. Then the LORD God made a woman from the rib he had taken out of the man, and he brought her to the man.' Now, whatever you think about how God did this, the whole emphasis is that men and women are the same. Here the word 'rib' can just mean 'side'. It is as if God took half of man and fashioned the woman. They are, therefore, the same. When the man sees the woman his response is: 'This is now bone of my bones and flesh of my flesh.' To paraphrase for a moment, it is as if Adam said, 'This is great! I've been lonely, but here is someone just like me.' So the emphasis is that men and women are the same.

The famous Puritan Bible expositor Matthew Henry has a very lovely way of putting all this as he comments on the passage. He remarks about the woman being made from Adam's rib: 'God did not make the woman out of Adam's head to rule over him, nor out of his feet to be trampled upon by him, but out of his side to be *equal* with him, under his arm to be protected and near his heart to be beloved.'

The emphasis again is on equality. There is an underlying sameness. Both are equal in the image of God. The great challenge which the church must take up is that in making room for the differences between men and women they should nevertheless feel that equality.

Male and female are two of a kind. But then, having said that, obviously they are different from each other. This brings us to the second answer that Genesis 2 gives to our question: 'What is woman?'

2. *Woman is different from man*

We are not talking about a stereotyped woman, let me remind you, but the archetype of what it means to be a woman that we find here in Genesis 2. What is she like? Let's look again at

Genesis 2:18: 'It is not good for the man to be alone. I will make a helper suitable for him.' For the man to be on his own is not quite right. God therefore makes man a companion who is like him, but different from him. Within the fellowship of the Trinity there are relationships between persons who are the same as each other, in that each one is God, but at the same time different from each other. The Father is not the Son; the Son is not the Spirit; and the Spirit is not the Father. The relationship between male and female will be something of an echo of this pattern.

The evidence that this is the case comes in the initial announcement by God of the creation of mankind. We read of God saying, 'Let *us* make man in *our* image' (Gen. 1:26, emphasis added). The 'us' and the 'our' used by God in referring to himself reflects his Trinitarian nature. Further, having mentioned that mankind will be made in 'our' image, the Genesis text goes on specifically to mention the two genders:

> In the image of God
>   he created him;
> male and female
>   he created them
>
> (Gen. 1:27).

In the New Testament the human relationships between those in the church are mentioned by Jesus as ideally being those which reflect the relationship between himself and his Father (John 17:21). But, of course, the first human relationship was that between Adam and his wife.

The woman was made as a 'suitable helper' for the man. The word 'suitable' can literally mean 'opposite'. How are men and women different? I am going to attempt to summarize this once again with three key words:

Help

God says, 'I will make a helper suitable for him' (Gen. 2:18).
The first key word concerning God's making a woman is the
word 'help'. Just as God made man for a purpose (we saw that
in the previous chapter — he made man to work the ground),
so God made woman with a particular purpose. As God made
the man to suit the purpose for which he intended him, so God
made the woman to suit the purpose for which he made her.
Archetypal woman is a helper. Let me just explore that a little.

First, *the word 'helper' in Scripture in no way implies any
disparagement.* How do I know? Because the same word 'helper'
is used of God himself many times in the Old Testament. For
example:

'My father's God was my helper'

(Exod. 18:4).

The eternal God is your refuge…
    Who is like you,
    a people saved by the LORD?
He is your shield and helper

(Deut. 33:27-29).

God is our refuge and strength,
    an ever-present help in times of trouble

(Ps. 46:1).

The LORD is with me; he is my helper

(Ps 118:7).

So there is absolutely no slur, no denigration, as that word is
used in scriptural terms. The woman is a helper and God too is
a helper.

Secondly, *to help someone implies being in a relationship
with that person.* You cannot help people unless you are in

contact with them. As Adam was taken from the ground to work the ground, so Eve was taken from Adam to help him. Genesis 2:7 speaks of the Lord God forming the man 'from the dust of the ground', but verse 22 tells us, 'The Lord God made a woman from the rib he had taken out of the man.' There is a parallel here. The man who works the ground is taken from the ground. The woman who helps the man is taken from the man. Men and women are the same, but there is a different focus. Femininity is to do with having a distinctive grasp of human relationships. The woman is a 'people person'. We will come back to that later. But relationships are a very important part of what it is to be female.

Thirdly, we have to say that *'help' is a general word.* Adam's task was very specific — to keep the Garden of Eden, to till the ground; it was a very focused task. Eve's task was much more diverse. To 'help' is more holistic and I think the Bible would encourage us to see women as therefore better at handling diversity than men. The woman of Proverbs 31 does so many things, doesn't she? She looks after the family (v. 15), she buys a field (v. 16), she looks after the poor (v. 20), she is able to spin (v. 13) — and all these things, and many more, she is able to handle. I want to suggest to you that part of femininity is to do with this ability to be able to cope with many different things simultaneously.

An article appeared in one of the UK broadsheet newspapers in 1999 by Anne Moir that underlined this. Research seems to show that male and female brains are actually 'wired' differently. Let me quote: 'The differences are visible in brain scans. When a man does a crossword puzzle, only the left side of his brain is active, but a woman … uses both sides of her brain while she solves the clues. And what is true of verbal challenges is true of much of life. Studies show that in general, the male's brain is focused while hers is more integrated. The female's brain is designed to do several things at once, whereas the male brain is more focused, more compartmentalized, more built to do one thing after another.' The article went on to describe an experiment in which six men and six women were asked to complete a series of tasks — wash up, brew coffee, make toast, scramble eggs, take a phone message and iron a shirt — in a limited time. The men failed. The result was a walk-over for the women.

The woman of Proverbs 31 is seen buying a field, ordering the affairs of the household, displaying wisdom, showing compassion and involved in trading. This woman is successfully carrying out multiple tasks. She is generally equipped to be a helper in every sense.

Nurture

Here is the second key word for woman. It is a small step from the idea of 'help' to the idea of 'nurture'. Nurture is helping others to grow.

For the male we have that word 'initiative', but here we have this word 'nurture'. In Genesis 2 we see that whereas the man's work was first of all focused on the garden, the woman's purpose is centred on the man. She was made a helper suitable *for him*. Women are, generally speaking, more people-orientated than men. This links back again to the experiment of the BBC TV *Horizon* programme which I mentioned in chapter 2. The boys in the experiment were more interested in the task, whereas the girls were more interested in their companions.

That nurture is part and parcel of helping and womanhood is seen in God's declarations after the Fall in Genesis 3. Man's identity is bound up with his working the ground, and it is the ground that is cursed (Gen. 3:17) because of his disobedience to God. The parallel for the woman is not only that her relationship with her husband becomes problematical, but that her pain in childbirth is increased (Gen. 3:16). The implication is that the identity of the woman is linked to the nurture of life. This is reflected again later in the chapter as Adam gives his wife the specific name Eve 'because she would become the mother of all the living' (Gen. 3:20).

Of course, our understanding here can also be linked to the fact that when God made us, the purpose for which he made us is reflected in the way he has constructed our bodies. 'Nurture' is very much part of femininity. The whole matter of nurturing a baby in the womb and feeding the child is built into the physical make-up of the woman. Whereas the man is strong particularly in his upper body, the woman is strong in the lower body for childbearing. So let's take up that word 'nurture' for a moment.

First, let me suggest that what God shapes in the physical side reflects something of what is there within us as well. What a woman is physically reflects what she is in her inner self. If this is the case, then the word 'nurture' is not taken as referring just to physical nurture, but to a whole attitude of nurturing which is portrayed as a feminine characteristic in Scripture.

Mary gave birth to Jesus, but she also seems to have been concerned to support him throughout his life. She is even there at the cross as he dies (John 19:25,26).

Other women, too, were involved in a supportive way with our Lord. 'Also some women who had been cured of evil spirits and diseases: Mary (called Magdalene) from whom seven demons had come out; Joanna the wife of Chuza, the manager of Herod's household; Susanna; and many others. These women were helping to support them out of their own means' (Luke 8:2-3). The Gospel writers draw our attention to the women who cared for Jesus' needs and encouraged the disciples.

Think of Paul as he writes Romans 16:2: 'I ask you to receive [Phoebe] in the Lord in a way worthy of the saints and to give her any help she may need from you, for she has been a great help to many people, including me.' Here is help and nurture. In verses 12 and 13 of the same chapter of Romans we read, 'Greet Tryphena and Tryphosa … who work hard in the

Lord. Greet my dear friend Persis, another woman who has worked very hard in the Lord. Greet Rufus, chosen in the Lord, and his mother, *who has been a mother to me, too*' (emphasis added). This woman had not given birth to the apostle Paul, but she had nurtured him; she had exercised some kind of spiritual maternal influence on Paul.

Single women too are nurturers. They can nurture other people in their personalities in whatever relationship they are to them. Maybe it is your friends. There can be that building up, that bringing out of their personalities. Maybe it is the boss? He or she needs to be encouraged, supported and caused to grow. That is the feminine attitude.

Let me make a suggestion in this area of nurture. I think many people have this generalized view that women do think differently from men and, as we have seen, there is scientific evidence which seems to support that idea. I think that is what lies behind Professor Higgins' song, 'Why can't a woman be like a man?' It may be that this matter of nurture explains that. We often speak of a woman's intuition. It is related to this. You will remember the mother of our Lord Jesus Christ, Mary. It is written of her concerning the things said of our Lord Jesus: 'Mary treasured up all these things and pondered them in her heart' (Luke 2:19). She took these things within her and turned them over in her heart. Again Peter speaks of the woman with a 'quiet spirit' (1 Peter 3:4). There is a nurturing of ideas suggested within her heart. It seems to me that there is something there in Scripture along those lines.

Sensitivity

In the narrative in Genesis 2 God makes the helper. God is making the one fittingly opposite to man, the partner for man. In this narrative the woman is defined, not just as opposite to the man, but also in terms of being different from the animals.

God brought the animals to Adam to name them and then we read, 'But for Adam no suitable helper was found' (v. 20). Perhaps we can imagine Adam saying to himself, 'These will not do. These are not good enough. They are not the same as me.' Therefore, when we come to the making of the woman, we must see her also as being different from the brute beasts. She is the one who fits the bill. These do not.

One of the implications here is surely that the beasts are insensitive and therefore inhuman. Woman has that required sensitivity. In one sense it is perhaps right to see woman almost as 'more human' than the man. Man's strength enables him to take the knocks and not feel them so much. But the woman is a little bit weaker and that means she feels more. She is more sensitive — not just physically; she is more sensitive in her spirit, and that takes us back to what we said earlier about this matter of relationships. The woman, the helper, is the one in relationships who is often sensitive. The woman has a special perception to see people's needs, to understand how they are feeling, to feel for them and thus to nurture them. Her sensitivity fits her for her function of helping, just as man's strength fits him for his function of working.

Think of that great Bible woman Abigail (1 Sam. 25). She was married to a foolish brute of a husband named Nabal. The word Nabal means 'fool'. He was an unthinking, selfish man. Nabal was being unfair. David had protected his property from marauders. But Nabal thought nothing of that and was unwilling to show any kindness to David, even when he was in need. David was angry. Abigail stepped into the situation. She knew her husband was wrong. She knew that David was right. She could feel what was going on in that relationship. She knew that it was going to end in disaster unless she stepped in and did something. She could feel what that brute of a man, Nabal, could not. She had insight. She was sensitive. It seems to me that Scripture says that it is particularly around such areas of personality that we locate femininity.

The influential helper

So the words which the Scriptures link with true femininity are 'helper', 'nurture' and 'sensitivity'.

God makes this gorgeous creature, Eve, and brings her to Adam, and what is his response? He sees Eve and bursts into poetry:

> This is now bone of my bones
>   and flesh of my flesh;
> she shall be called 'woman'
>   for she was taken out of man'
>
> (Gen. 2:23).

Adam is thrilled. He is stimulated and the comment goes on to say, 'For this reason a man will leave his father and mother and be united to his wife.' He is stimulated to do that by coming into contact with the woman. She moves him. This is the woman's 'strength'. The female has great power to stimulate and attract men, first of all by physical beauty. It is not wrong for women to care a little about that, just as it is not wrong for a man to want to keep himself strong and physically fit. A woman must not make an idol of her looks, but it is not wrong to care about what God has given. God made woman as the 'glory of man', according to 1 Corinthians 11:7.

But woman can also stimulate man by that feminine heart, that feminine spirit within which is so different from his and which is, as it were, mysterious and fascinating to him and therefore tremendously attractive. The apostle Peter locates true beauty as an inward virtue. Speaking in a comparative way, he says, 'Your beauty should not come from outward adornment, such as braided hair and the wearing of gold jewellery and fine clothes. Instead, it should be that of your inner self, the unfading beauty of a gentle and quiet spirit, which is of great worth in God's sight' (1 Peter 3:3-4).

That is femininity. Woman, the sensitive helper and nurturer, therefore has great power with respect to men. Perhaps one of the reasons for Satan's strategy, in the events leading up to the Fall, of approaching the woman first lies here. It was not because the woman was in any way inferior to the man, but because he knew she had not heard the commandment directly from God, as Adam had, and he knew that Adam was so attracted to his wife. Satan knew that if he could get a hold on the woman he would have a very good chance of getting hold of the man too because Adam was so attached to her.

Women have a great power when it comes to men. And, women, it is your responsibility to use that power for *good* in people's lives.

We have considered 'helper', 'nurture' and 'sensitivity' as words which particularly seem to spell out the essence of biblical femininity. But, finally, just as we said with the male, all this is in the context of the word 'obedience'. Woman, like man, is to be obedient to God. What we have seen emerges from Genesis 2, which describes the situation before the Fall. This word 'obedience' once again must undergird all these things we have seen.

A definition of femininity

So, having done some Bible homework, we can come to a kind of definition of femininity. This definition is not to be taken rigidly and inflexibly. But it is to be seen, as it were, as the centre of the orbit of femininity. Obviously genuine femininity can express itself in many different ways. We must allow for different personalities and different gifts in different women.

God does not want us all to be precisely the same. But with our definition we are trying to specify the centre of the orbit around which femininity revolves. We have arrived at a definition that goes like this:

> At heart, mature femininity is a disposition to sensitively receive, help and nurture others in ways appropriate to a woman's differing relationships.

Think about that. Obviously an unmarried woman and a married woman have different relationships with men. The woman who is married to a particular man has a special relationship with him that is different from relationships with other men whom she comes across in her life. She must therefore keep within the appropriate channels of relationship. She must not treat all men as she would treat her husband. Neither must she treat her husband or her son as she would any and every man. But, appropriate to the relationship, she has that disposition to sensitively affirm, receive and nurture. A mother can help her son. She can encourage her husband. She can help others. The single woman can encourage friends, others in the church, or at the place of work. She may want to act as an extra 'auntie' to various children. Such is the variety of our relationships in society, the extended family, the workplace and the church that we must be left to think for ourselves as to what time and effort should be invested in each relationship.

Relatively speaking

Let me say again that these distinctives, which it seems to me are there in Scripture, are to be taken relatively. It is not that men cannot be sensitive. Nor is it that they cannot nurture in their way. They can because men and women are the same.

We are human. But in the female these things form the centre of the orbit. These virtues come to the front of the stage. The distinguishing marks of masculinity are to do with work, sacrifice, initiative and strength. These things are the centre of his orbit. But in the woman help, nurture and sensitivity form the focus. These have a greater prominence.

Secondly, we have talked about the image of God. Let me say how I think this is to be understood. Men and women are equally in the image of God. That is the case first and foremost because both men and women are capable of personal relationships with their equals, in love and truth. This reflects the relationships within the Trinity.

In particular, the image of God is linked with the capacity for language — foundational to relationships. The succession of human generations in Genesis is a succession of names. This is different from the animals. On the opening page of our Bibles we find a God who speaks and, made in his image, both male and female equally have the gift of language.

However, some people might not be satisfied with that answer. They may say, 'That is fair enough, but if God reveals himself as "he", how can woman be equally in the image of God?' It may be that the answer is precisely because she is not 'he'. Adam is made in God's image but God is *not* a man. Here we are confronted with divinity. There is an 'otherness' about God. God is not a man and woman is other than man. This is the balancing factor. Thus she is equally the image of God.

If we can accept that, it would immediately explain why the apostle Paul in Romans 1 associates homosexuality so closely with idolatry. Turning away from the true God, worship is directed to foolish idols, and Paul's logic quickly jumps from there to homosexuality. Homosexuality is love of the same rather than love of the other, and to worship idols is to worship the creature — the same — rather than the Creator, who is other.

They go hand in hand. However we argue it, the Bible is clear
that women and men are equally in the image of God.

Let me say another provocative thing. While I know that
there are many very difficult circumstances and particular situations, and while I have every sympathy for women who are
encouraged by our secular society and go ahead with abortion, we can see that abortion is the very opposite of nurture. If
what has been proposed as being the distinguishing features of
femininity is true, then abortion is the very antithesis of womanhood. That is why it is a lie that you can have an abortion and
just shrug it off as if it means nothing. Many women find they
cannot do that because it actually is an attack upon their femininity. It is an attack at the very root of what you are as a
woman. Just as we said before that to take work away from a
man is an attack upon his masculinity, so I would say this about
abortion. I understand that there are many difficult circumstances
and we need sometimes to be sympathetic and realize that there
is forgiveness with God, but God's Word teaches that it is not
right to take innocent lives.

Men, can you see the pressures that are here upon women?
Christian men must encourage Christian women. Let us be all
that we should be as men towards them. We should act with
respect, care and sacrificial love towards them so that as they
stand, or seek to stand, for biblical womanhood, which the world
despises, they might know they are not despised by us. They
must be made to know that they are greatly honoured for being
women as Scripture would have them be. We must help one
another.

Application

We conclude this chapter by asking how to be a true woman.
The answer, of course, is to be with God. Just as we have already

seen, a man was only a true man in Eden before the Fall, before his true masculinity was distorted. And to be a true man he must go back to God. In just the same way, to be a true woman is to go back to God. It begins with walking with God, for him to shed his love, his forgiveness and his Holy Spirit into our hearts that we might have the strength through our relationship with him to be what we ought to be in our relationships on earth. That feminine way is what you as a woman were made for. Therefore take God's Word within you. Think through what has been said in this chapter, and receive whatever you find the witness of your conscience and God's Spirit telling you is of God. God says, 'Here is my Word; take it within you. Receive the life of the Lord Jesus Christ into your life; welcome him into your life; become a Christian if you are not one already. Receive the gospel, the forgiveness of sins through Jesus Christ through following him. Receive the new life of the Holy Spirit and nurture that within your life.' That is the way to find the power to walk with God. That is the path of true femininity.

Questions

1. From what you have read in this chapter, in what areas are women better than men?
2. In the light of what we have seen about what makes a good woman, take time to read through Esther chapters 1-7. Compare and contrast the characters of Vashti and Esther. List examples to follow and to avoid.
3. Read Proverbs 31:10-31. List all the phrases which speak of the value of a good wife. Write a few sentences which summarize the outlook of the woman mentioned here.
4. This chapter argued that the female emphasis is to do with help, nurture and sensitivity. If you are a woman, think through your own personality and life situation and decide practical ways in which you could be more feminine in the biblical sense.

4.
Head of the family

Ephesians 5:21-33

Let me begin with a couple of Bible verses. In 1 Corinthians 11:3 Paul writes, 'Now I want you to realize that the *head* of every man is Christ, and the *head* of the woman is man, and the *head* of Christ is God' (emphasis added). Again, in Ephesians 5:23 he says, 'For the husband is the *head* of the wife as Christ is the *head* of the church, his body, of which he is the Saviour' (emphasis added).

What is this headship business? In particular what does the Bible mean when it says, 'The head of the woman is man'? Obviously it is a controversial subject. We live in a society, sadly, where the phrase 'the battle of the sexes' has been coined. It seems that men and women relate to each other less and less in respect and service. Instead we now have the gender wars.

In this situation such verses as those quoted above are explosive. Families can be divided, churches can be split and individuals can fall out over the issues involved. But there are enormous misunderstandings and misrepresentations and misuses of what the Bible says concerning this matter of male headship.

It has been said, 'A lie can be halfway around the world before the truth has got its boots on.' That is right. It certainly seems true in this matter of what the Bible teaches about the relationship between men and women. Distortions and falsehoods in this matter often fuel the flames of controversy. This subject is extremely controversial. However, I think we can go to the crux of the topic by asking two simple questions. They are: 'What does the Bible teach?' and 'What does it *not* teach?' No doubt some will dismiss this as too simplistic, but please stick with me.

What does Scripture teach about male headship?

We focus on Ephesians 5:21-33:

> Submit to one another out of reverence for Christ.
>
> Wives, submit to your husbands as to the Lord. For the husband is the head of the wife as Christ is the head of the church, his body, of which he is the Saviour. Now as the church submits to Christ, so also wives should submit to their husbands in everything.
>
> Husbands, love your wives, just as Christ loved the church and gave himself up for her to make her holy, cleansing her by the washing with water through the word, and to present her to himself as a radiant church, without stain or wrinkle or any other blemish, but holy and blameless. In this same way, husbands ought to love their wives as their own bodies. He who loves his wife loves himself. After all, no one ever hated his own body, but he feeds and cares for it, just as Christ does the church — for we are members of his body. 'For this reason a man will leave his father and mother and be united to his wife, and the two will become one flesh.' This is a profound mystery — but I am talking about Christ and the church. However, each one of you also must love his wife as he loves himself, and the wife must respect her husband.

This is a passage concerning Christian marriage, but it is still of value to you if you are single, for you will see later in the chapter how it relates to you too.

'The husband is the head of the wife as Christ is the head of the church, his body, of which he is the Saviour' (v. 23). There are at least six things here in this passage concerning male headship.

1. The context of headship

Look at verse 21. Flowing out of the Spirit-filled life there should not only be praise, but mutual submission: 'Submit to one another out of reverence for Christ.' Mutual submission, putting others before ourselves, is something to which all Christians are called, but it is that which defines the larger context and sets the tone for all that follows: 'Submit to one another out of reverence for Christ.'

We can see immediately that, with that text forming part of the context, male headship has nothing to do with male oppression and unfeeling dominance over women. In many ways that is the opposite of what Paul has in mind. True headship is not an easy job. Rather it is almost as if the husband has to say, 'Out of submission to my wife, I'll take this difficult job of headship!'

'Submit to one another' (v. 21) again assumes the fundamental equality of male and female. God made them both in his image (Gen. 1:27). Men and women have different roles but are equal partners, with equal value. That is obviously there from this verse which defines the context.

We are to have this attitude of submission towards one another 'out of reverence for Christ'. We are to do this out of respect for the Lord who saved us. This way of servanthood is *his* way. He who was in the very form of God made himself a servant and humbled himself and became obedient to death

(Phil. 2:5-8). Furthermore, it is his command to us that we take this attitude, and we owe him reverent obedience. He is our God who loved us and gave himself for us. Adopting such servant-like attitudes is the way to worship him and bring him honour in our relationships. That is the context in which Paul introduces this matter of headship, and we are not to miss that.

2. The metaphor of headship

What role model are we to take as men to pattern ourselves on? 'For the husband is the head of the wife as Christ is the head of the church... As the church submits to Christ, so also wives should submit to their husbands' (Eph. 5:23-24). Christ is the only pattern of true headship on whom we are to model ourselves. Any other ideas from other sources are not relevant and are unhelpful. Christ alone is the role model for true male headship. That means two things.

First, *there is a responsibility and an authority in the husband* that should be respected (v. 33). Christ does have authority over the church. Much as our present Western culture does not like that idea, we cannot take that out. In the sight of God a husband does have an authority over his wife. He is responsible before God for his family in a way that his wife is not.

But, secondly, we have to see that *the pattern of the exercise of that authority is the way of Jesus*, and no other. 'You know that those who are regarded as rulers of the Gentiles lord it over them, and their high officials exercise authority over them. Not so with you. Instead, whoever wants to become great among you must be your servant... For even the Son of Man did not come to be served, but to serve, and to give his life as a ransom for many' (Mark 10:42-45). Yes, there is true authority in Christ and therefore in the husband. But this way of Christ is the only true pattern for the exercise of that authority. The world treats with respect those who stamp their feet and shake their fists.

They treat servants with disrespect. But Christ is the Servant Master, isn't he? He is the one who gave himself for us. There is the metaphor of headship for the husband. The husband therefore deserves respect as he takes that way of Christ.

3. The practice of headship

We have already begun to touch on this. It must be said that the practice of male headship demands all your manliness, to love your wife with all strength, perseverance, initiative and self-sacrifice. We have this spelled out in verse 25 which reads: 'Husbands, love your wives, just as Christ loved the church and gave himself up for her to make her holy, cleansing her by the washing with water through the word, and to present her to himself as a radiant church, without stain or wrinkle or any other blemish, but holy and blameless.' How did Christ love the church? Paul takes us to the cross. Christ let what happened at Calvary happen to him, for the sake of his bride! He sacrificed himself completely for her to save her. And, husbands, you are called to that same kind of sacrificial headship — not another sort of headship, but that kind of headship.

Christ did all this when the church was far from what he desired her to be (v. 26). He did it in order to make her holy when she needed cleansing. He did it when she was stained and blemished. Christ loved us 'warts and all', not because everything about his bride was perfect. Husbands, you are called to a Christlike love, a Christlike headship. Jesus did it to bring his bride, the church, to utter fulfilment and joy to the glory of God, 'to present her to himself as a radiant church, without stain or wrinkle or any other blemish, but holy and blameless. In this same way, husbands ought to love their wives as their own bodies' (vv. 27-28).

Some of us have to ask ourselves, 'How many wrinkles and furrows have we put into the brows of our wives through an ungodly headship?' Christ's love is fulfilling, designed to take away the wrinkles, to make her radiant and free and fulfilled, to present her to himself radiant. Does our love make our wives radiant, so that they feel free and fulfilled and blessed? Christ is the head of the church. He took the dirty job in order to bless his wife, to the glory of God. If you are a husband then you are the head to do *her* good.

On most occasions when a man and wife are walking sub-missively with Christ they will agree about any decisions that are to be made. With the husband's initiative, and talking the matter through, they will come to an agreed conclusion together.

But sometimes the man, as the head of the house, has to make the final decision in a situation where the way ahead is not clear, or where his wife disagrees. At that point he must listen lovingly to his wife. This does not mean that he must always do as she would like, but he must understand her fully. He may honestly come to the conclusion that what she desires would not be for her ultimate good, or the good of the family, or the glory of God. In such a case he must lovingly stand firm. But he is to make the decision on the basis of what he prayerfully feels would be for his wife's good and the glory of God. The point is that the husband is called to sacrifice. He is never to use his immediate personal desires as the basis for his decision-making. Why? It is because Christ did not come to please him-self. He came to do the will of God and to save his bride, the church. Every decision he made was for the glory of God and the good of the church. In Gethsemane he prayed, 'Not my will, but yours be done.' And that is the practical model of head-ship that husbands are called to follow.

Now that does not mean that no man is ever blessed through his marriage. Far from it. We shall look at how a man is blessed in marriage later in the chapter. But we see that Scripture actu-ally gives women far more rights than any feminist liberation movement. Scripture gives the woman the right to be loved sacrificially. Scripture lays the command for self-denying, self-giving love upon the man. Wives, of course, do love and give sacrificially. But for a husband it is his first duty. Women are not first called to sacrifice themselves for their husbands, but their husbands are called to sacrifice themselves for them so that a wife might find genuine freedom and bloom and be radiant as a woman. That can happen as a woman finds herself so loved. As it dawns upon her, 'I am so valued by this gallant man,' she finds fulfilment. She can find herself being transformed, just as the church is transformed by the love of Christ.

In the introduction to this book I quoted a heart-cry from Harriet Taylor Mill which expresses the concerns of so many women. In the quotation she asks, referring to women, the fair question, 'why the existence of one half of the species should be merely ancillary to that of the other ... there be nothing to compete in her mind with his interests and his pleasure'. We should be able to see by now that it is not simply many women who question such a state of affairs. Scripture itself deplores such a situation. The Bible exalts women. There is a male head-ship within marriage, but it must be a servant headship, which serves and blesses the woman. Just as Christ, the head of the church, is the great servant of the church, so a husband who is the head of his family must be the servant of his family. And that will often mean putting his own 'interests and pleasures' to one side for the good of his wife.

4.The motive for headship

We have already seen that both partners in the relationship should act out of reverence for Christ. However, the passage does point to another motive. Although Christ did not make decisions on the basis of his own wants but, rather, in sub-mission to God, on that of the needs of the church, yet, of course, the ultimate outcome of that is his own delight. He is now able to present the church to himself in all her glory (v. 27).

Here, too, is the way of the husband's blessing in marriage. As he puts his wife's good first, the husband will find himself more than rewarded. 'In this same way, husbands ought to love their wives as their own bodies. He who loves his wife loves himself. After all, no one ever hated his own body, but he feeds and cares for it' (v. 28). The motive is that she is part of you and will be a blessing to you.

Really what Paul is doing here is going back to the Genesis 2 story. You remember that Eve was created from the rib taken out of the man. She was the same body as Adam, and no man ever hated his own body. They come together again and become one flesh in marriage. Christ's bride is in union with him and in a sense the church is part of Christ. She is a blessing to him, or should be. She certainly will be in the future new creation. So, for us who are husbands, our wives are part of us and are a blessing to us. And for us to mistreat our wives is to bring problems and trouble back to ourselves. By contrast, being a blessing to them will result in a blessing to ourselves! There is the motive which legitimately guides a true head of the family.

5.The response to headship

How is the wife to respond? The wife is to 'respect her husband' (v. 33). To respect the man the wife must submit to that man's love. 'Wives, submit to your husbands as to the Lord' (v. 22). Wives are to submit, not foolishly, for a wife's first responsibility is to the Lord, not to her husband. But she is to submit to his love and his attempts to do good to her, and for the Lord's sake to back him up and support him, even when he does make mistakes. Wives are to do this to the glory of God, thanking the Father that he has commanded that they should be so loved. When a wife responds to her husband's love in such a way, it will help her husband. He will feel valued and that will spur him on in his task of costly, self-giving headship.

6.The theatre of headship

What is the stage on which this headship acts? What is the
sphere in which it operates? It is within the bonds of marriage.
Paul is very specific in verse 24: wives are to submit to their
own husbands. They are to submit to their *own* husbands in
the Lord. So it is not true that all men have authority over all
women. Paul is saying, 'This is within marriage. You submit to
your own husband. It is not for another man to start seeking to
lead you.'

As we have seen in previous chapters, true masculinity is
predisposed to care for and work for the good of all women
(and other men). Similarly, true femininity is inclined to help
and nurture all men (and other women). But this must be in
terms of what is appropriate to the relationship. Headship and
submission are mentioned by Paul as being appropriate to the
marriage relationship, not to any other.

A biblical definition of headship

Gathering all these things together, it seems we can come to a
definition of what Scripture teaches concerning male headship
like this:

> In the marriage partnership of two equals before God,
> man and woman, the man bears the primary responsibil-
> ity to lovingly protect and sacrificially lead the relation-
> ship in the direction of God's glory and the woman's good.

How does this apply outside the family?

We have touched on this question before, but it is worth return-
ing to it. What about man-and-woman relationships outside

marriage? For example, what about if I am at work, I am a single woman and come into contact with other men? What if I am a married man and in church I am on a committee with a woman who is someone else's wife? How are relationships of this kind to work out?

We have to say that full-blown headship does not apply there. Paul has been speaking about marriage. But we must also say that its potential is meant to be preserved. There is no specific authority/submission directive in such relationships. But, nevertheless, the same attitude is to be preserved. If what we have seen about masculinity and femininity is true, then archetypal masculinity is suited to this kind of servant headship which we have seen in marriage. And archetypal femininity is suited to be responsive and nurturing towards such a servant head. Therefore in our various daily contacts with different people, because we are male and female, that is to be respected and to be noticed, not ignored.

Scripture does not say that in a workplace a woman should never be the boss. Lydia was a well-off business woman. Probably she had men who worked for her. In the early church many male Christian slaves would have been answerable to the mistress of the house. Scripture doesn't say that was wrong. It doesn't say a woman should not be a headmistress in a school with male teachers, or that she should not be a consultant doctor with male junior doctors under her. But I think Scripture would encourage that even in those situations there are ways of respecting the essence of masculinity and femininity.

Here is a woman who is a boss of a firm of solicitors or accountants. Obviously she would need to call a meeting and lead the proceedings. But there are ways that she can acknowledge the maleness of the men under her and they can acknowledge her femaleness. So on the way to the meeting a man might open the door for her, or he might offer his chair where there is that particular situation. Again the way the conversation around the conference table is conducted should be

such that men present show a regard and a protectiveness towards the boss. Gentlemanly courtesies of that kind on the part
of the male are to be received positively on the part of the
female. Obviously such courtesies may vary in different cultures. What we would do in England might not be the same as
we would do in Kenya, or Amman, or wherever, but those attitudes are to be preserved as the male seeks to be the servant
protector. And these courtesies should be joyfully and happily
respected and accepted by the woman, so that in a sense all
women should feel like VIPs in the company of mature Christian men, and Christian men should feel that they are doing
good to all Christian women.

Again, take another situation at work. The woman may or
may not be the boss, but that woman may suffer from sexual
harassment. It is a matter of mature masculinity to protect her
and to step in appropriately and not to let her be exposed to
that. That is what a mature Christian man would do. What kind
of attitude is God after? I think 1 Timothy 5:1-2 is a good text
for this situation. Paul writes to Timothy telling him how he
should handle different relationships: 'Treat younger men as
brothers, older women as mothers, and younger women as
sisters, with absolute purity.' Let us reflect. How should a man
treat his mother? He will treat her with respect and with protectiveness. How ought a good mother to respond to that? She
will respond pleasantly and with joy and acceptance. Similarly
how should a man act towards a sister? He will act with respect
and with protection and care. And how should a sister respond
to that? She will respond with happiness, gratefully receiving
such kindness. The woman is not to brush it off with an 'I don't
want this; I don't need you,' type of comment.

So those male and female attitudes outside of marriage can
be rightly respected and preserved. It seems to me that this is
the direction in which Scripture would lead us as we ask the
question, 'What does Scripture teach on this matter of male

headship?' and apply it both within marriage and outside marriage.

What Scripture does *not* teach about male headship

Having set out the positive teaching, we must knock on the head a few errors which are around today and have the effect of undermining the biblical teaching. All the objections raised in this section are errors to avoid, so please don't take them the wrong way! Here are five errors to avoid.

1. 'The Bible does not teach male headship at creation'

That is not true. It does. It is seen in many different ways. For example, Genesis 1:27 tells us:

God created man
    in his own image,
in the image of God
    he created him;
male and female
    he created them.

The generic name for the human race is what? *Man!* That is not just a tradition; that is how God put it in his Word. God chose that. It is indicative of a male headship.

Again in Genesis 2:7 Adam was made the first of the royal family of the human race that God brought into being. This, as we have already seen, is indicative of the initiative/leadership aspect of masculinity.

Or again in Genesis 2:17 we find that it was Adam who was commanded and held responsible for his race not eating the forbidden fruit.

Genesis 2:23 speaks of Adam, having named the animals and thus showing his headship over creation, naming the woman. He names her with the most exalted name, indicating that she is utterly equal with him, but he still names her. This once again reflects his headship over her.

The teaching of Genesis 2:24 is that when it comes to marriage the male leaves his parents' family. He initiates the new household. This is the responsibility of the head. It is clear, then, that male headship is right there at creation. It is an error to say headship is not part of the original perfect creation.

2. 'Male headship is the result of sin'

That is not true. Remember the account of the Fall in Genesis 3. It is because Adam was already the head, and therefore held responsible, that he was held responsible for the Fall, the entry of sin, even though we find in Genesis 3:6 that Eve ate of the fruit first: 'When the woman saw that the fruit of the tree was good for food and pleasing to the eye, and also desirable for gaining wisdom, she took some and ate it.' Adam only ate later. But he is blamed; he is held responsible. Why? In Scripture the coming of sin upon the whole human race is never blamed on Eve. You never read, 'As in Eve all die...' You do read, 'As in Adam all die...' You do read, 'Sin entered the world through one man, and death through sin' (Rom. 5:12). Adam's headship already existed prior to, and was not consequent upon, the Fall.

All of the human race, even Eve herself, came from Adam. She was taken out of him. Adam is like the trunk of the tree and we are the branches and twigs, and when the trunk of the tree fell, we all fell with him. It is not true that male headship is a result of the Fall.

However, what is true is that male oppression and a wrong female response to male headship are the result of the Fall. After the Fall God says to the woman:

I will greatly increase your pains in childbearing,
    with pain you will give birth to children.
Your desire will be for your husband
    and he will rule over you

                                                        (Gen. 3:16).

In other words, 'Because of the way human nature has become
corrupted by the entrance of sin, you will both react wrongly
from now on.' That word 'desire' in this verse is used again in
Genesis 4:7. When God speaks to Cain, who is upset that God
has not accepted his sacrifice, God says, 'If you do what is right
will you not be accepted? But if you do not do what is right, sin
is crouching at your door; it desires to have you.' Sin desires to
control Cain. Women will respond like that to men and men,
because they are sinners, will respond by seeking to oppress
women.

So what is true is that this great distortion and misuse of
male headship came in at the Fall. It was that terrible distortion
away from Christlike headship to dominance and oppression.
It was away from the servant headship of Christ. Male headship is not the result of the Fall. It is the *misuse* of headship
which stems from the Fall.

3. 'You cannot have headship and equality at the same time'

'If there is headship it must mean that the female is less than
the male.' That is what some people would say. But it is not
true. How do I know it is not true? We read in 1 Corinthians
11:3, 'Now I want you to realize that the head of every man is
Christ, and the head of the woman is man, and the head of
Christ is God.' If you are saying that you cannot have headship
and equality at the same time, then your logic must lead you to
conclude that Christ is less than God and you are moving away
from orthodox Christian teaching on the Trinity. The Father is
the head of Christ, but Christ is equal with God the Father. This

is what Scripture teaches. To say that you cannot have equality and headship leads to a fundamental attack on the truth of the Trinity. John 1:1 tells us, 'In the beginning was the Word, and the Word was with God.' John goes on to say, 'The Word was God,' and 'The Word became flesh and made his dwelling among us. We have seen his glory...' (John 1:1,14). So such an idea rejects the very foundations of the faith and it is very interesting that many radical feminists have left the church over the last thirty years to pursue a New Age spirituality, which rejects Christian teaching on the nature of God.

Or look again at another text, Galatians 3:28. In his letter to the Galatians Paul is defending the gospel of justification by faith alone. He is thinking of what it is to become a Christian. He says in this context, 'There is neither Jew nor Greek, slave nor free, male nor female, for you are all one in Christ Jesus.' Paul obviously believed that in Christ male and female are absolutely equal. All are one in Christ Jesus. Yet Paul is the same one who wrote Ephesians 5 and says, 'The head of the wife is the husband.' Is Paul being inconsistent? Had he jettisoned what he said to the Galatians by the time he wrote to the Ephesians? Of course not. He knew what he was talking about. If you say, 'You can't have both headship and equality,' then what you are saying is that you know better than the apostle Paul.

4.'The word "head" has no connotation of authority and responsibility'

Some scholars have been promoting this interpretation in recent years. In the ancient literature on some occasions the word 'head' may just mean source. We sometimes speak of 'the head of a river', for example. But the overwhelming use of the word has distinct connotations of authority. This is obvious from Ephesians 1:22, which reads, 'And God placed all things under [Christ's] feet and appointed him to be head over everything for the church.' It is not just that Christ is the source of salvation for the church; he has authority over the church. The very definition of a Christian disciple as one who 'follows' Christ, and submits to him as Lord, implies this. Let me say again, his authority, his headship, is not oppressive. It is the Servant King who is head over all. But he does have authority over the church. He is the head.

5. 'Headship of the male in Scripture is purely cultural and not a fundamental teaching'

'It just happens to be that the New Testament was written in a culture where men were looked upon as the head of the household. Now our culture has changed and we can forget it!' That is the approach of some people.

I will admit that the expression of headship may vary legitimately in different cultures. But the idea that headship itself is purely cultural is not true. It is rooted in creation, going right back to Adam and Eve, as we have seen. It is, in a way, pre-cultural. It is part of the creation order from the beginning, and God's redemption is about restoring the creation order, not abrogating it. We are restored in the image of God. Thus in Ephesians 5 Paul does not argue from the customs of the day, but from Genesis. He expounds what it means to say that male and female are one body. The same can be said of other passages. Paul's words in 1 Corinthians 11 link male headship to the relations between the persons of the Trinity. The truth of the Trinitarian nature of God is not dependent on any temporal earthly culture. As Paul discusses the roles of men and women in the church in 1 Timothy 2:11-15, again he argues, not from the prevailing social norms of the city of Ephesus where Timothy was located, but from the Genesis account of the creation and the Fall.

Perhaps these errors have not yet come the way of some readers, but I am trying to deal with them here so that if and when you do come across them you will have already thought about them and will be prepared for them.

We have seen, then, something of what Scripture teaches and what Scripture does not teach on the subject of headship. We must now ask a further question that we have often asked in this book.

Why is this subject important?

The subject of headship is crucial at two levels.

1. At the everyday practical level

This teaching of Scripture enables male and female relationships to be beautiful and fulfilling and not contentious and battling. Here, in a husband, is the head who loves his wife and gives himself for her, and here, in a wife, is one who is happy to submit to that love in the partnership of two equals before God.

This teaching enables women to be respected. Women in our society are attacked and abused simply because they are weaker and because this kind of teaching has been thrown out by our contemporaries. But throwing out this teaching does not change the fact that, generally speaking, women are physically weaker than men. Throwing out this teaching does not change sinful human nature that is prepared to exploit any weakness.

Sadly, our culture in the West has changed for the worse. Whereas fifty years ago most of our towns and cities were safe places for women at night, that is now no longer true. Women have become prey, partly because Christian attitudes have been rejected. It is looked upon as old-fashioned to be a 'gentleman'. If the teaching of Scripture were taken on board women would be safe in our society and free to be what they want to be. They would be free to walk home in safety along dark streets. They would be free to be cared for and cherished. The biblical teaching also gives man the proper outlet to express his energy and masculinity, not in violence and rape and ugliness, but in giving himself, sacrificially, strongly, taking the initiative for the blessing of women in a way that is appropriate to the relationship. We submit to one another out of reverence for Christ. It is practical and it is beautiful and it helps at an everyday level.

But headship is also very important from a gospel point of view.

2. At the level of salvation

How are we saved, Christian? The answer is because we have a Head, who is responsible for us, who has authority over us and who properly represents us before God. Our Head is the Lord Jesus Christ.

In Adam, our original head, we all fell into sin because of his rebellion against God. He represented us then. But in Christ all who are joined to him by faith are saved because he lived a righteous life, because he died on the tree for our sins, on our behalf. It is not because of anything we have done, but because of what he did. What he has done for us at Calvary, he did as our Head. 'Christ is the head of the church, his body, of which he is the Saviour' (Eph. 5:23).

Let us take an example. Here is a man who has lived a great public life and has done many great things, and he is made a duke. And here is a woman who has lived an ordinary life and done none of those great things, and she marries this man. She becomes a duchess. She does so, not because of anything that she has done, but because she is joined to her husband. She benefits from his achievement. How do we become saved, have our sins forgiven and become heirs of God? Not because of anything we have done, but simply because we belong to him who has done everything. We benefit from his achievement because he is our Head. It is all free to us as we are joined to him by faith.

How are we saved? The answer is, because we have a Head. We have a Head who loves us and represents us. To undermine this matter of headship is, if we are not careful, to undermine the way of salvation itself.

It may seem, superficially, that to insist on the idea that the husband is the head of the family is to make a fuss about nothing and to defend a relic of Victorianism which really ought to be consigned to the waste bin of history. But what is ultimately at stake is far more important than many people realize. To tamper with the biblical teaching on headship is actually to tamper with the gospel itself. Nothing could be more serious.

Questions

1. Read through the six chapters of Ephesians noting all the verses which mention the word 'head' in some way. You should find five. Bearing in mind the context, from the use of the word in Ephesians write out your own definition of what the word means.
2. Look at Ephesians 5:21,25. In what sense is a husband's headship a way of submission?
3. Look at Ephesians 5:27. How ought Christlike headship in a husband to make the wife's role a joy? How ought church-like submission and growth in a wife to make a husband's role fulfilling?
4. Although Christ is our example of biblical headship, we are sinners and he is not. Describe some ways in which husbands can misuse their headship. What might be the consequences of such behaviour for the wife and the rest of the family?
5. What do Luke 15:17-21 and Luke 17:3-10 teach about how to seek and how to grant forgiveness?

5.
The church as family

1 Timothy 3:1-16

In 1 Timothy 3 Paul calls the church 'God's household'. He says, 'If I am delayed, you will know how people ought to conduct themselves in God's household' (v. 15). The church, of course, is not a building. Colloquially people speak of the church when they mean the building, but that is not a true understanding of the word 'church' in the New Testament. In New Testament terms the church is the gathered Christian people. And in writing to Timothy, who is looking after the church at Ephesus for a while, Paul calls the local congregation there 'God's household', or 'God's family'.

We have been looking at what Scripture says about male and female as created by God and redeemed by him. In the previous chapter we looked at Ephesians 5 in particular. We saw what the Bible teaches about male headship within a marriage. We saw its authority and its servant nature.

Now we come to look at what Scripture says about male and female within the church, and as we do this we shall see that this concept of the church as 'family' is particularly important. It is with this underlying thought of the church as a family that Paul handles the matter concerning roles of men and women within the church. The ordination of women, especially into the 'priesthood' of the Anglican Church, has provoked discussion and captured news headlines throughout the last twenty-five

years, and continues to do so. As this book is being written, the
grapevine is suggesting that it will not be too long before we see
the first women bishops. All this provokes a stir in the churches.

The family nature of the church

The church as family is a big theme that runs throughout the
New Testament. God is 'our Father'. As Christians we are 'born
again' into God's family; we have become 'children of God'.
These are all New Testament terms that we know well. This
terminology of the Christian life and the idea of the local church
as family are woven deeply into all the New Testament letters
and are found here in 1 Timothy.

If you look at 1 Timothy chapter 1, you will see that in this
passage Paul calls Timothy 'my true son in the faith'. Timothy
was not only God's son but Paul's 'son', in that it was through
Paul that Timothy had been converted to Christ. He had been
born again as the Word of God had come to him through Paul.
Later the term 'brothers' arises in the same letter. Paul writes,
'If you point these things out to the brothers, you will be a good
minister of Jesus Christ' (1 Tim. 4:6). And that word 'brothers', of course, springs up again and again in this epistle and
many epistles in the New Testament. It is a word which includes
the idea of both brothers and sisters, so that some of the gender-
sensitive modern versions of the Bible actually include the words
'brothers and sisters' quite legitimately in the translation of
1 Timothy 4:6, and elsewhere. People who are Christians in
the church together are siblings. It is a family word again.

The whole family is called to love one another. 'The goal of
this command is love, which comes from a pure heart and a
good conscience and a sincere faith' (1 Tim. 1:5). And we could
go through many, many such texts in the New Testament which
encourage us to love one another in the church as family
members. In 1 Timothy 5 Paul is giving advice to the church

about how to handle situations where perhaps a family are not able to look after their older relatives. Paul is saying that in this situation the church should take up responsibilities for older members, stepping into the family's shoes when the family of relatives cannot cope. The church is to be a family to the older person in this very practical way.

A particularly important text in this epistle is 1 Timothy 5:1-2, which we have already mentioned in the previous chapter. But we refer to it again because it stresses the family nature of the local congregation. Paul says, 'Do not rebuke an older man harshly, but exhort him as if he were your father. Treat younger men as brothers, older women as mothers, and younger women as sisters, with absolute purity.' Family terminology is used concerning how to behave towards one another, particularly within the church. We relate to one another as if we were a family together. This fleshes out the practical implications of being a member of God's household.

We treat the members of our families in special ways. So in 1 Timothy 5:1-2 we find Paul telling us that we *must* treat older men like fathers and the younger women like sisters. We must do this, not only because in some general sense we must love them, but because this particular attitude is appropriate to the kind of family relationship that we have with one another in the church. Conduct towards other members of the family must take into account not just the general obligation to love, but the concrete distinctions of being different kinds of family member.

Let me spell it out. I must love my wife and I must love my daughter, but *not* in the same way! I must love each of them in particular ways. My love to my wife should include romance, but that would be inappropriate towards my daughter. I must love my daughter in a paternal way, but too much paternalism towards my wife could be misconstrued as patronizing and unhelpful. It may appear that I am implying that she is lacking in maturity.

Likewise also with my father and my sons. I must love them all, but not precisely in the same way. My love for my father must include an honour and a certain deference for his seniority. But my love for my sons is to be such as to build them up while at the same time gently encouraging them to show a proper deference to me, their father, in accordance with God's command to honour your father and mother. They are treated differently.

Similarly, Paul is saying that this kind of logic works within the church. How do we treat older women? Well, we are to treat an older lady as if she were our mother. That is, we treat her with an affectionate deference. How do we treat younger women? We are to treat them as if they were our sisters. There should be a protective, loving equality. How do we treat that older man? We treat him as if he were our father. That is what Paul is getting over to us here. Fellow church members are to be treated like fellow family members.

Once we see that, we see that what we learned in the last chapter about roles within a family simply cannot be discarded in the context of the church and we cannot say, 'This is irrelevant to ecclesiology.' What we learned about roles within a family has to be appropriately and sensitively transposed into the life of the church. We wish to see every gifted woman and every gifted man used well in the church of God, but this preservation of the relationships of the family just cannot be overridden when it comes to male and female roles in God's church. So this brings us to our second heading.

The family structure of the church

Before we go further, I need to spell out that in the New Testament the leadership of the church is split into two groups. There is the eldership and there is the diaconate. The elders and the deacons are mentioned together in Philippians 1:1. The pastor, or minister, is elsewhere referred to as the teaching elder. He is to be seen as simply an elder, but one who is set aside specifically for the public teaching of God's Word.

1 Timothy 5:17 speaks of 'the elders who direct the affairs of the church', or who 'rule' the church. Elsewhere Paul speaks of them as being 'over' the congregation in the Lord (1 Thess. 5:12). They have, as they use the Word of God, an authority within the church.

The deacons are somewhat different. 1 Timothy 3 tells us that the deacons serve: 'They must first be tested; and then if there is nothing against them, let them *serve* as deacons... Those who have *served* well gain an excellent standing...' (vv. 10,13, emphasis added). If you carry out a search of the New Testament you will see that the word that attaches to eldership is the word 'rule', whereas the word that attaches to the diaconate is the word 'serve'. As those who follow the Lord Jesus, the elders must, of course, exercise a servant rule. They are to lead for the good of God's people, not their own good. But there is an authority about eldership (Heb. 13:17), which is not attached to the diaconate. With this in mind, elders in the New Testament are sometimes called 'overseers' (e.g. Titus 1:7).

The word 'deacon' comes from the word for 'table servant'. There is nothing derogatory about the term. The Lord Jesus himself came not to be served, but to serve (Mark 10:45). So there is a distinction between elders and deacons. Elders direct the affairs of the church; the deacons particularly serve. We understand from Scripture that the deacons are a 'general help' to the elders as they seek to lead and direct the affairs of the church (see Appendix I).

That, in a nutshell, is what the New Testament teaches. How does this matter of family then impinge upon what we have said about the matter of the leadership of the church?

When we think in terms of family relationships being transposed into the church, there are three things that suggest themselves when we consider the roles of men and women.

1. Just as husbands and fathers ought to exercise godly servant headship in their human families, so wise mature *men* ought sacrificially to lead the church as *elders*.

2. Just as wives and mothers ought to nurture and support male headship in their human families, so good, godly *women* ought to be the *helpers* of male leadership in the church.

3. Just as parents in a family have many duties and joys in common and yet the respective functions of male and female are *not* reversible in the family, so they are not reversible in the church.

Having stated this, we fill it out from what is taught in 1 Timothy. We are going to talk about male headship and we are going to talk about female help.

1. Male headship

We begin by reminding ourselves of our definition of headship that emerged in the last chapter:

In the partnership of two equals before God, man and woman, the man bears the primary responsibility to lovingly protect and sacrificially lead the relationship in the direction of God's glory and the woman's good.

In Paul's teaching this carries over into the church. Elders direct the affairs; they teach the church. We read in 1 Timothy 2 that 'A woman should learn in quietness' (v. 12). Then again Paul says, 'I do not permit a woman to teach or to have authority over a man; she must be silent. For Adam was formed first, and then Eve.' Paul is not speaking about the culture of his time; he is talking about what God did at creation. He is linking his ideas right back to Genesis, so that his teaching is built into the whole history of relationships.

Then he goes on to verse 14: 'And Adam was not the one deceived; it was the woman who was deceived and became a sinner.' Speaking about the Fall, Paul is pointing out that the roles of male and female were reversed as Eve took the initiative to eat of the forbidden fruit. She ate the fruit and Adam followed her. Paul is using this fact to underline that for women to take authority over men in spiritual issues is wrong. Eve took a decision without referring to Adam and it led to disaster. Adam's headship was overridden, and Adam followed Eve in eating the fruit. Thus they all fell together. For women to take the role of authoritative teachers within the church is to be deceived.

Paul concludes verse 15 by asserting that the 'helping' and 'nurturing' role of the woman is of paramount importance. 'But women will be saved through childbearing — if they continue in faith, love and holiness with propriety.' He focuses upon the particular matter of childbirth but behind that, as we saw in chapter 3, is this whole helping and nurturing aspect that we have spoken of before as being so close to the essence of femininity. So the taking the role of helper and nurturer which is frequently despised by the world will not in any way have an adverse effect upon a woman's relationship with God. A woman can use all her gifts and intelligence in that supportive, helping role, without needing to usurp authority. Salvation is not a matter of teaching, or climbing some imaginary ladder of hierarchy within the church. It is a matter of faith in Christ, love to others and holy living. Here then, quite clearly, Paul asserts male headship in the church.

As we would expect with such an important matter, this is not the only place in his letters in which the apostle made this plain. The troubled church in Corinth faced the question of how male headship relates to the church. In the opening half of 1 Corinthians 11 Paul tackled this subject (vv. 3-16). It is a complicated passage but the main thrust of it can be summed up quite simply. Although not giving authoritative teaching, women can positively participate verbally in church worship given certain conditions. The condition for female participation is that the headship of the male should be respected and that it should be *seen* to be respected in public worship (vv. 6-10). This is the point of the head-covering that Paul refers to in this passage. He positively wants the women to be fully involved, but in a way which preserves the same headship structure in the church as is present in the family.

The assumption of male leadership in the church undergirds 1 Timothy 3:1-5, where Paul begins to answer the question: 'How does a church choose someone for eldership? What qualifications are required?' Paul says, 'If anyone sets his heart on being an overseer, he desires a noble task. Now the overseer must be above reproach, the husband of but one wife...' Already Paul assumes a male eldership, for he speaks of the elder as 'the husband of but one wife, temperate, self-controlled, respectable, hospitable, able to teach, not given to drunkenness, not violent but gentle, not quarrelsome, not a lover of money. He must manage his own family well and see that his children obey him with proper respect. (If anyone does not know how to manage his own family, how can he take care of God's church?)'

Immediately you can see the link-up there. Paul has already mentioned the family and the church family. Paul is saying, 'One of the things to think about when considering whom to appoint for eldership is to look at how the man is leading his own family.' If he has done well and served diligently in the context of his own family, then there is good reason to believe that he is going to give the same kind of diligence and care and bring the same kind of blessing in the family of the church. That doesn't mean necessarily that all elders *must* be married. Paul himself and the Lord Jesus were not married. But Paul is simply assuming that generally speaking settled men will be married. The assumption here is that of male eldership.

In 1 Timothy 3:12 Paul brings a similar kind of test for deacons but it is especially pressed home with respect to eldership. That man — has he been the kind of Christlike, servant head of his family? Then the church is to reflect the structure of the family and makes that practical link. How has he done in the family? That is a good indication concerning his potentialities in the church. There you can see why the church traditionally down the years has taken the position of male headship in the church. It is not a matter of raw male chauvinism. It is a matter of the church being a family. This brings us to the second heading relating to the family structure of the church.

2. Female help

The parallel between family and church helps to clarify this whole area of a woman's role within the congregation of the church. Consider the situation within a natural family. We may find within a family a variety of skills and gifts. A wise husband and father will encourage the development and use of those abilities to the fullest within his family. Good elders will follow the same pattern within a church.

Headship, properly understood, is enhanced, not threatened, by the full flourishing of the whole family. A wise husband will learn from his wife and be very blessed in so doing. A wise husband gives many responsibilities into the hands of his wife (Proverbs 31 is a case in point). We need our wives' help in the family. We need women's help in the church. Management is in many ways a shared responsibility throughout the whole family, with the child perhaps having special responsibility to keep his room tidy. In a family a wife may have a much better head for finances and figures than her husband. It is not wrong for that responsibility to be deputed to her. We all have different responsibilities and in that way are all involved in management. But the father nevertheless exercises overall authority over the household as a whole.

It is meant to be similar within the church. It seems to me that Paul begins to say something about this here in 1 Timothy 3. Look at verse 11: 'In the same way, their wives are to be women worthy of respect.' The word there for 'wife' can just as easily be translated 'women'. Thus we have: 'In the same way, the women are to be women worthy of respect.' I do not think that the women referred to in this verse were the deacons' wives. The commentator William Hendriksen says that is clear from the syntax. If you look at the three categories — 'elders must be...', and then 'deacons, likewise...', and then, in verse 11, 'the women in the same way...' — it is as if he is dealing with three categories. What he says is that there were a group of women who helped the leadership. Call them deaconesses if you like, but they were a group of women who helped the leadership. They didn't contend for leadership for themselves, but helped the leadership at every level. They were not elders, but they helped the elders. They were not called deacons, probably for the simple reason that the Greek word for deacon/servant has no feminine form. Thus Paul simply refers to them as 'the women'.

Just as for a good family, the husband needs the help and support of his wife without her trying to wear the trousers, so for a good church the male leadership needs the help and support of women at every level. They need women involved with helping the elders, involved among the deacons, specifically set apart by the church to do that, without trying to reverse this business of male headship. So women need to be involved at every level, but without trying to threaten God-ordained male leadership, the reasons for which we have seen in previous chapters (see Appendix II).

It makes sense that there should be, as it were, mothers in the church — for example, that there should be mature women able to counsel women under the authority of the eldership.

Let me say that a 'mother' in the church doesn't have to be a married person. She can be a single lady. In the congregation where I serve we used to have among us a dear retired missionary called Edith who was obviously a 'mother in Israel'. In her younger days she had run an orphanage in north India. What a great blessing to us she was, with all her great experience of the Lord in years gone by! Women are to teach other women, says the New Testament, particularly on matters that relate to living as a Christian woman (Titus 2:4). Women can help and advise in an untold variety of ways.

The Jewish people of Jesus' day took this matter of male headship and misused it. Women seem to have had very little involvement in the synagogue. Christ rejected that. Christ had women who were with him, helping him. I believe that is partly how we should understand the story involving Martha and Mary in Luke 10:38-42. Martha was busy in the kitchen, and that was fine, but she seems to have perhaps had the mentality which says, 'I'm in the kitchen doing this — Mary, you don't need to be learning theology, you know. Forget it; you should be where the women's place is, in the kitchen.' 'No', says Christ, 'that is not true.' Women are needed in all the ministry of the church. Women need to learn theology in order to bring a female perspective and to help the leadership without seeking to usurp the male authority. Just as wives work alongside their husbands within a marriage, so women and men work together within the church.

It seems to me that here we have the balanced nature, the balanced structure, of the family as it is to be reflected in the local church.

We have seen the 'family nature of the church' and the 'family structure of the church' and now there are one or two things we need to consider under the heading of application.

Application

Firstly, can you see *the wisdom of this?* Suppose the church has a different set of roles from the family. Surely that is going to put some people in impossible situations. Here is a husband whose wife is the pastor or the elder; how can he be the head of his house? Is he talking to his wife, for whom he is responsible before God, or to his elder, who is responsible for him before God? Or think of the situation of a single daughter and her father. Suppose the daughter is an elder in the church and is still living at home under the father's roof. How is she to relate to her father, and how is he to relate to her?

No, the reversing of the family roles in the church would put people into impossible positions in their families and in fact will begin to threaten the structure of the family at home. So the wisdom of Scripture is that the structure of the church reflects the structure of the family at home so that they can fit together.

That seems to lead to a general principle about the church and the family. The church and its ministry should never seek to overrule the rights and duties God has entrusted to families, but rather to support and nurture them.

Here is a new convert: perhaps a lady has been converted; she is born again. This has happened to her as a married woman and she may say, 'But I'm married to this man who is not a Christian, who doesn't want to know about Christ,' and may jump to the conclusion: 'Let's get a divorce!' Scripture says, 'No, you must support your husband.' The Christian wife is to stay. If the non-Christian husband wants to go that is a different matter (1 Cor. 7:15). But the church should always do its best to support families.

Those working among young people are always, and only, to encourage youngsters in loyalty and love to their own families. We are to build up the families within the church. Here in 1 Timothy 5, it is true that the church will look after elderly relatives, but Paul's great emphasis in that passage is to encourage the family to do it first because it is their God-given responsibility. He is supporting the family. Can you see that principle? I am not saying that you are to neglect the family for the church. Nor am I saying that you neglect the church for the family. What I am saying is that God has shaped these things so that they fit together easily. They are structured to fit together rather than oppose one another.

The second thing that comes by way of application is that the proper functioning of leadership and help in the church depends for smooth running on *the developing and nurturing of a family atmosphere and love and respect for one another in the church*. If a church is nothing more than a preaching station it is way out of line with the vital Christianity of the New Testament. If all that people ever think about when they think about the church is some man standing at the front who speaks, they will conclude that preaching is the only thing that matters in the church. If this is the case, obviously women, and others, will say, 'Why can't I do that?' and the tensions will build up. This can be simply because Christians are making preaching the be-all and end-all of what a church is. Scripture says the church is to be a family. Of course, preaching has a big part to play, but it is only a part of what the church is about. There are ministries in so many different areas because we have got to look after one another as a family.

There are fathers and brothers in the church, but there are also mothers and sisters in the church, and the leadership needs the help of the 'mothers' in the church. The women will find that they can be used to the fullest in such a church. The church must be a real family together. There is to be a holistic view of people. We have physical and emotional needs as well as spiritual needs. Just as the Lord Jesus healed the sick and fed the hungry alongside his preaching of the good news, so ministry within the church is to be a looking after one another in every possible way. Unless we have that kind of commitment to one another and vision of what a church can be, it will not work. There will be tensions that build up which should not be there simply because people have no avenues in which to express their God-given gifts of ministry. We must submit to one another in brotherly love, honouring one another above ourselves. All of us are included in the ministry of the church family.

Thirdly, by way of application, we need to ask each reader, 'Are you a member of God's family?' The church is a family. It is God's family. True freedom and dignity are found, not in self-assertive, self-centred choices, and rebellion against the way we have been created. *True freedom flows from becoming a child of God.* It comes from repentance and renewal of our inmost being by the Holy Spirit. When our hearts are so changed through faith in Jesus Christ we come to find that the commands of God and the way he has structured our lives are not a burden, for we have begun to think like our Father in heaven.

That is not to say that we shall always find his ways easy as Christians. When an adopted child enters a new family he or she will take time to learn the ways of the new family. Sometimes it will seem easier to cling to old patterns of behaviour that we were familiar with before we became Christians. Change can be difficult. But, nevertheless, those who have turned from their old life with a new heart of thankfulness to follow the Saviour, who died to take their sins away, will deep down want to respond positively to God's commands. As we find ourselves doing that, in practical areas of life such as those we have considered in this book, it is a sign that we really have become God's children.

There is an incident in the Gospels which helps us to understand what it is to be part of God's family. We read, 'Now Jesus' mother and brothers came to see him, but they were not able to get near him because of the crowd. Someone told him, "Your mother and brothers are standing outside wanting to see you." He replied, "My mother and brothers are those who hear God's word and put it into practice"' (Luke 8:19-21).

Perhaps as you have read this book you are not a Christian. God invites you to join his family and get involved in the church. You matter to God. God looks upon you as one who is lost and without hope, who is worth saving, to whom his heart goes out. God would summon you. You must respond. That response means that God is to come first in your life as you put your trust in Jesus Christ. God becomes your Father, and Christ your Elder Brother. Christ died that your sins may be blotted out and that the new life of the Spirit might be given to you.

The Bible says of Christ, 'He was in the world, and though the world was made through him, the world did not recognize him. He came to that which was his own, but his own did not receive him. Yet to all who received him, to those who believed in his name, he gave the right to become children of God — children born not of natural descent, nor of human decision, nor of a husband's will, but born of God' (John 1:10-12).

Questions

1. Read through 1 Timothy. List as many ways as you can find in which God's church is like a family.
2. How would you describe the difference between the roles of elders and deacons in a church? (See, for example, Acts 6:1-6; 1 Tim. 3:1-13).
3. Why do male church leaders need help from women ? (Rom. 16:2: Phil. 4:3). What are some of the practical dangers when male leaders refuse to have any input or help from mature Christian women?
4. This chapter and Appendices I and II argue that it is perfectly scriptural to appoint women deacons. What do you think about this and why?
5. The word 'deacon' is tied up with the idea of service. Read Philippians 2:5-11. Why does sincere Christian service carry a great dignity?

Appendix I
The deacons: A brief summary of the biblical teaching

As churches we, from time to time, look to God our Father for guidance concerning appointments to the diaconate of the church. In doing this it is essential that we have a clear grasp of the Bible's teaching relating to deacons in our minds.

1. The scriptural basis for the office

When Paul wrote to Timothy to explain how local churches are to be ordered (1 Tim. 3:14-15), he mentioned the two offices of elder and deacon. The setting out of requirements of character for the deacons and the fact that candidates were to be tested by these requirements make it clear that the diaconate was a definite office in the church to which people were appointed (1 Tim. 3:8-13).

In writing to the church at Philippi, Paul includes the elders and deacons specifically in the opening address of the letter (Phil. 1:1).

It seems clear that, although the office of deacon was filled by men, there were also women specifically appointed by the church to act alongside the deacons. It is very unlikely that 1 Timothy 3:11 refers to deacons' wives, as there is no similar reference to elders' wives. The Greek word here simply means 'women' (see also Rom. 16:1; Luke 8:2-3).

Why do we have deacons? Not because it is traditional; not just because it is a pragmatic expedient; but because the Word of God says that such an office should be set up for the well-being of the church.

2. The origin of the diaconate

The beginnings of the diaconate should be considered in two ways.

Theologically

The glorious, ascended and reigning Lord Jesus Christ gives gifts to his church (Eph. 4:7-13). Every gift is for the good of the church and is a direct expression of the love and concern of Jesus for his church. In Romans 12:7, *diakonia* is listed among the charismata.

Historically

The diaconate in embryo is to be found in the opening verses of Acts 6. Although these seven men are not specifically called 'deacons', yet the task to which they are called, 'serving tables' (Acts 6:2), is the root meaning of the word 'deacon' (e.g. John 2:5). The fact that Stephen and Philip were engaged in evangelistic preaching simply shows that we should be careful not to circumscribe the functions of the diaconate too rigidly. It is, then, in the context of church ministry to *the needy* within the fellowship that this office arose (Acts 6:1-3).

3. The functions of the diaconate

The general distinction between the eldership and the diaconate is that the elders are to *rule* well (1 Tim. 5:17), and the deacons are to *serve* well (1 Tim. 3:13).

The word 'deacon' *(diakonos)* in Scripture is inextricably bound up with the idea of service (Mark 10:45; Luke 10:40; 22:26-28; Col. 1:23,25).

While all the members of the church are to seek to care for one another, the New Testament focuses this aspect of service on the diaconate to ensure that this ministry is fulfilled within the church.

In Scripture it seems that an eldership is set up in a church before the diaconate (Acts 14:23; Titus 1:5), and then, as the work develops and elders require help, deacons are appointed. In the broadest sense the diaconate is the helping hand to the eldership, and we are to see the deacons as those who generally facilitate the practical function-ing of the church.

In Acts 6 the seven chosen were used of God to:

- set free church leaders from practical difficulties and attendant distractions (v. 2);
- set free the community of the church, delivering it from want and squabbling (vv. 1,3);
- set free the Word of God. The seven took on those legitimate areas of church concern which, if performed by the apostles, would have taken time from prayer, study and ministering ('deaconing') the Word. Acts 6:7 is the practical result of the work of the seven.

4. The qualities required in a deacon

1 Timothy 3:8-13 sets out six requirements of character for those to be appointed to the office of deacon. They are to be:

- persons worthy of respect or honour, noble, dignified, serious (v. 8);
- not double-tongued, insincere, saying differing things depending on whom they are speaking to (v. 8);
- not given to much wine, not addicted or controlled by their appetites (v. 8);
- completely honest, not fond of dishonest gain (v. 8, cf. 6:10);
- having a firm and sincere grasp of the fundamental truths of the gospel (v. 9);
- having an exemplary family life (v. 12).

Candidates must be tested in such areas (v. 10).

5. The significance of the diaconate

The diaconate stands as an eloquent and permanent witness to God's concern for the whole person. The church is not to be exclusively interested in a person's soul, but in all that he or she is as a human being (James 2:15-16; 1 John 3:17). This has evangelistic implications, too.

The diaconate stands as an eloquent and permanent affirmation of the centrality of preaching and prayer in the purposes of God (Acts 6:3-4; Titus 1:3).

The diaconate stands as an eloquent and permanent reminder of the necessity of practical order, efficiency and innovation in the work of the church. The church is to exercise not just natural prudence, but Holy Spirit wisdom (Acts 6:3; Eph. 5:16).

Appendix II
Women deacons: an explanation of the New Testament passages

What is said here is not original to me. It owes much to a paper given at a study conference of the British Evangelical Council on the role of women in the church.

Introduction

No one can object to women (or men) doing works of service, for this is simply to act as a Christian. The point at issue is whether there is biblical warrant for women occupying diaconal office within the church.

Background

Both Old and New Testaments teach that men and women are equal (Gen. 1:27; Gal. 3:28). Both Old and New Testaments teach male headship within church and family (Josh. 24:15; 1 Cor. 11:3; Eph. 5:22-24). These principles must be upheld.

The New Testament sees elders as 'ruling' the church, under the supreme authority of Christ (1 Tim. 5:17), whereas the deacons are the designated helpers of the elders, 'serving' the church (1 Tim. 3:13).

Relevant New Testament passages

The relevant texts which touch on women and the diaconate are
Romans 16:1 and 1 Timothy 3.

1 Timothy 3:1-13

The passage moves from speaking about *elders* (v. 1) to *deacons*
(v. 8) to *women* (v. 11) to *deacons* (v. 12). The problem is to estab-
lish what Paul meant by *gunaikas* in verse 11. Linguistically it can
mean either 'women' or 'wives'. There are five possible options. These
are that the word refers to:

1. women in general;
2. wives of elders and deacons;
3. wives of deacons;
4. women deacons;
5. a group of women similar to deacons but distinct from them.

The context and location of verse 11 within the passage make options 1 and 2 extremely unlikely. If he meant number 3 — deacon's
wives — Paul could have made this plain by specifying '*their* wives'
— but instead of using the possessive, he just speaks of 'women/
wives' (v. 11).

Furthermore, the phrase 'in the same way' (v. 11) parallels the
'likewise' of verse 8 (both *hosautos*), and, significantly, the qualifications for the *gunaikas* and the deacons parallel each other.

Deacons (v. 8)	*Gunaikas* (v. 11)

must be:
worthy of respect	worthy of respect
sincere (not double-tongued)	not malicious talkers
not indulging in much wine	temperate
not pursuing dishonest gain	trustworthy in all things

All this points to these women *(gunaikas)* being officers alongside the
male deacons. But, it may be objected, why did not Paul call them
'deaconesses'? The answer is straightforward: he is writing in Greek,

not English, and the feminine word did not exist for him. *Diakonos* (deacon/servant) was used for both men and women in the secular world of the time. If Paul wanted to speak distinctly of *women* deacons and to specify the qualifications for them analogous to those for the men, he would need to speak of 'the women' *(gunaikas)*.

Romans 16:1

Here Paul plainly uses the word *diakonos* of a woman, namely Phoebe, from the church at Cenchrea (part of Corinth). He has no problem with attaching the word to a woman.

Some seek to argue that Paul is speaking generally of 'service' in the church, not of Phoebe as holding an office of deacon in the church. But though there is some dispute among commentators, the Greek grammarians favour the view that Paul is speaking of an office. The particular genetival construction which Paul uses points in that direction.

Conclusion

Seeing deacons as helpers to the elders means that male headship within the church is not breached by the appointment of women deacons, and from what we have seen the New Testament evidence is that women did hold such positions in the early church.

Appendix III
Work, family and church?

A brief survey of problems which Christians experienced in connection with working life was carried out in my own congregation. The biggest problem which emerged was in the area of balancing time for work, family and church. Similar surveys in two other churches, one in London and the other in Lancashire, gave the same result.

In Britain people work longer hours than anywhere else in Europe. Six million people here work more than forty-eight hours a week. This is two million more than in the 1980s. The fastest growing group of long-hours workers is women, with an increase of two-thirds over the last fifteen years. At the end of the 1990s the Labour government brought in the Working Time Directive, which is meant to give employees the right to refuse to work more than forty-eight hours a week, without being penalized for so doing. It remains to be seen whether or not this will actually change things. On present evidence, it looks doubtful.

Long hours at work

Working long hours may bring high financial rewards or promotion to some people (Prov. 14:23), but there are definite problems.

Health

Overwork can lead to high blood pressure, sleeplessness and even heart attacks. According to BBC's *Panorama* programme in 1998, if people persistently work for more than forty-eight hours a week, say over a period of five to six years, their health will be permanently damaged. Statistics show that even if they then reduce the number of hours they work, they can never fully recover.

Family and relationships

Long-hours working leads to family tension and insecurity in relationships. Britain has the highest divorce rate in Europe and some experts think this is not unconnected to working practices. In recent research two-thirds of people working more than forty-eight hours a week reported that most days they did not speak to their children and that they have difficulty in managing them.

Spiritual life

The Bible encourages hard work (Gen. 1:27-28; Acts 20:35), but it promises blessing to those who take time to spend with God (Ps. 1:2-3; Isa. 40:29-31).

How should we respond?

Stress and pressure are helpful up to a point. God does intend us to face challenges and to work hard. He does not intend us to be lazy (2 Thess. 3:11-15). But if we feel ourselves acutely pressurized because of the demands of work, what should we do ?

There is no universal answer, or once-for-all cure. It is something we need constantly to look at and come back to. Here are ten suggestions to help think the matter through in a biblical way.

Five things to avoid

1. Avoid the idea that says only work matters. Biblically all three areas of work, family and church are priorities (e.g. Eph. 4:16; 5:22 - 6:9). If you do not see this, or play off one at the great expense of another, you will certainly run into trouble.

2. Avoid the world's outlook on ambition. Check the legitimacy of your ambitions in the light of Scripture if you are driven to work long hours by your aspirations (1 Tim. 6:9; 1 Thess. 4:11-12).

3. Avoid thoughtlessness. Is the pressure you are suffering simply due to a lack of proper organization of your life? Self-control can bring release from bondage. Surveys show that some people are happier at work than at home, and this could be because they feel better in a more orderly and structured environment. Perhaps our whole life needs more structure.

4. Avoid perfectionism. We do need to do our best for God at work and to do all to his glory (1 Cor. 10:31), but the Lord is not a slave-driver. He is easy to please. Reflect on Luke 22:28 in the context of the frequent failures by the disciples.

5. Avoid the "macho" spirit that equates being able to work long hours with strength and manliness. This often has its roots in an ungodly pride, which wants to show off to others.

Five things to do

1. Seek a basic and workable routine in your life. Genesis tells us that God has made us to follow a rhythm of life. He made night and day (Gen. 1:5). He also gave the weekly Sabbath to be kept as a day of rest (Gen. 2:2). If we reject these routines we shall suffer.

2. Review your priorities and if possible do it in co-operation with your spouse or with a friend. Set out where your priorities should be for work, family and church, and then compare them with where your priorities actually are. Then pray and talk through together ways in which the real priorities can move towards the ideal ones (Prov. 27:17).

3. Learn to discern between truly important items and those which clamour for urgent attention, but actually are not so important. This is one of the great secrets of the way the Lord Jesus was able to complete the work God had given him to do (Mark 1:35-39; John 17:4). Such discernment is very often gained through prayer and getting things in proper perspective by spending time in God's presence.

4. If the acute pressure is actually due to the company's making unrealistic demands upon you, and no amount of reorganizing yourself will alleviate things, then in some countries *you may have support from the law.* For example, in Britain you have the option of using the Working Time Directive, to take a stand that you work no more than forty-eight hours. You may need to consult a trade union, or a Christian organization such as Keep Sunday Special or the Christian Institute, to help you.

5. Some people decide on the radical step of *downshifting.* This means consciously seeking a new way to earn a living which does not require so much time. Often this decision will mean having to accept a lower salary, but such a move can lead to more enjoyment and a higher quality of life. This is not for everyone. It is a radical step and needs to be thought and prayed through carefully. But it could be the right way for some Christians.

The Bible, not least in the story of the exodus from bondage in Egypt, shows that our God is a God who is concerned with justice in the workplace (Exod. 3:7; Prov. 16:11). We should take seriously bringing our concerns about balancing work, family and church to him in our prayers (James 5:4).